Plan

**Ideation Skills for
Improvement and Innovation Tomorrow**

John Canfield
with Greg Smith

Black Lake Press
TELL YOUR STORY
BLACKLAKEPRESS.COM

Black Lake Press

TELL YOUR STORY
BLACKLAKEPRESS.COM

Cover design by Greg Smith of Black Lake Studio.

Published by Black Lake Press of Holland, Michigan. Black Lake Press is a division of Black Lake Studio, LLC. Direct inquiries to Black Lake Press at *www.blacklakepress.com*.

ISBN 978-0-9839602-2-5

Author's Note

Dedicated to the thousands of my clients who had the courage to wonder, change, and improve their workplaces.

The *Good Thinking Series'*, Part One: *Think or Sink. A Parable of Collaboration,* was a story, a narrative, an easy read.

Parts two and three, *Collaborate* and *Imagine,* and this book, *Plan,* are instruction books, and hence more like recipe books or repair manuals. As such I believe the reader will benefit more from completing the exercises and applying the tools and techniques immediately. Just reading the text will not provide the learning and benefit available from actually practicing with the tools and techniques with your own data, around your own issues, and seeing and applying your own results.

Chapters 1,2, 8 and 9 of this book, *Plan,* are very similar to the same chapters in *Imagine.* The core chapters of *Imagine* and *Plan* present useful ideation skills in different areas. *Imagine* covers process improvement and creative thinking skills.

Plan covers strategic planning and scenario planning. Strategic planning provides an opportunity for a senior team to discuss and decide what they want their organization to accomplish. This book will introduce and practice a ten-step process, ten great questions, that guides a senior team to learn what it would prefer to do.

Scenario planning helps teams consider alternative futures and prepare a successful response plan no matter what the situation. The alternate views will help generate new insights about a company and its possible futures. Thinking this way helps prepare contributors to notice and consider emerging ideas before others even perceive any change.

Scenario planning is an excellent complement and second step to effective strategic planning. This may even be the first time these two powerful planning methodologies have been presented together in the same book.

Table of Contents

Introduction

The *Good Thinking Series* is intended to help its readers significantly improve their organization's performance. The first book in the series is *Think or Sink: A Parable of Collaboration*. This book follows three leaders (a *competer,* an *accommodator,* and a *collaborator*) as they work to complete a major project. We learn about how these three leaders think and behave, how their supporting teams think and work for the team, and the likely business impact of these three leadership strategies.

The second book in the series is *Collaborate: Tools and Techniques for Better Meetings.* This book helps readers learn how to think, behave, and lead as a collaborator.

Both of the third and fourth *Good Thinking Series* books explain collaboration strategies designed to generate better ideas in specific areas of need:

The third book in the series, *Imagine:Ideation Skills for Improvement & Innovation Today,* helps leaders learn to understand and use specific idea-generating skills (Process Improvement Skills and Creative Thinking Skills) that help users generate tactical ideas for both improvement and innovation.

This fourth book in the *Good Thinking Series* is *Plan: Ideation Skills for Improvement & Innovation Tomorrow.* It helps leaders learn to understand and use specific idea-generating skills (Strategic Planning and Scenario Planning) that help users generate strategic ideas for both improvement and innovation.

	Tactical	Strategic
Improve (Convergent)	Process Improvement Skills	Strategic Planning
	Collaboration Skills	
Innovate (Divergent)	Creative Thinking Skills	Scenario Planning

The Importance of Ideas

Idea generating skills are crucial to an organization's success. They are the stepping stones to decisions and support. Implemented well, the ideas are transformed into improved business performance.

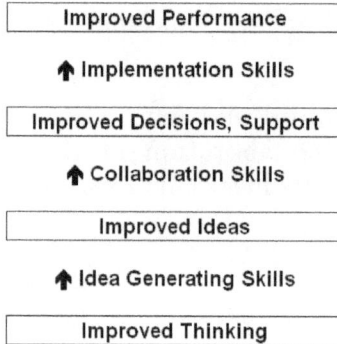

Improved Performance

⬆ Implementation Skills

Improved Decisions, Support

⬆ Collaboration Skills

Improved Ideas

⬆ Idea Generating Skills

Improved Thinking

Considering that you cannot realize what you cannot imagine, your ability to realize improved ideas can differentiate you from your competitors. Considering that you cannot will yourself a new idea, your ability to purposefully imagine improved ideas on demand can differentiate you from your competitors. The *Good Thinking Series* of books helps leaders and employees learn to think more effectively in a wide range of situations. The series helps leaders and employees learn to think more effectively on purpose, on demand.

Some Additional Helpful Ideas About Generating Ideas

Marvin Weisbord has developed a concept he calls *equifinality*. It describes a situation in which there is likely more than one way, one idea, that will support a given set of goals. There's more than one way to do things successfully. This takes the stress off finding *the* right answer. Rather, try to find three solutions to a problem. Then pick one and work hard to make it a success.

Joseph Juran coined the phrase "the Pareto Principle, the 80/20 rule," argued that among many ideas, a few will provide dramatic results. This idea helps us target the significant few, and leave the trivial many until later. You don't need to have a long to do list in order to be successful. In fact, you don't want to, because a long to do list is counter-productive to success.

Learning and using the approaches and techniques found in the *Good Thinking Series* is like taking ownership for the software on your computer, and not letting random programs confuse or derail your work efforts. The series is written to introduce the fundamental topics. There are many great resources to help you once you have actually started successfully. My main interest is helping the many company leaders and employees who have not yet started to make their thinking purposeful and effective. Either they've tried and failed, or they just have not found a resource to help them move from where they are and begin building momentum with their new thinking.

After decades of studying a wide variety of organizations around the world, I've come to the following conclusion: few of the many thousands of companies currently operating have shown that they have the thinking skills and discipline to successfully implement and maintain the benefits of the many improvement strategies available. I've written this series of books to help leaders begin or review a topic and then successfully implement the thinking and skills of productive collaboration and realize the benefits in their organization.

Resistant Leaders

Good Thinking Series, Part 4, Plan: Ideation Skills for Improvement and Innovation Tomorrow is a book for beginners. Beginners who want to learn how to ideate, how to develop more ideas when they need them. This book is also for those who are not satisfied with their previous encounters with these two topics and want to begin again.

The tools and techniques in the *Good Thinking Series* are not intended to replace the less formal processes that work for companies. They complement them. I am certainly not suggesting companies stop doing what's working. I am suggesting that companies work hard to continue to improve on what is working to remain competitive. I am suggesting that companies using tools and techniques will very much broaden both the number of options they can generate, and the number of employees who can help in problem solving and creative work. A company's next improvements and innovations may be hiding at the boundaries of their comfort zone. The *Good Thinking Series* is one resource to help companies raise the bar.

"The exact contrary of what is generally believed is often the truth."—Jean de la Bruyère

1

Ideation—Restraining and Promoting Considerations

The Merriam-Webster dictionary defines *ideation* as, "The capacity for or the act of forming or entertaining ideas."

When we are on an idea search, we are on a scavenger hunt for alternatives. As the iceberg diagram below attempts to show, not all the ideas we'd like to consider are above water, on the table, available to be discussed.

Ideas:

Know - Share

water line

Know - Don't Share

Know - Forgot

New - Thought for the First Time Ever

In a team environment, the ideas we know and share (above the water line) are often politically correct. This is similar to "weather talk" in the Stage Theory of Team Development (the "form/storm/norm/perform" model that Bruce Tuckman first described in 1965). Below the water line, "under the table," are many ideas that we share in confidence. These ideas are deemed not so politically correct, even politically dangerous, and often introduced with words that hint at a deeper meaning: "Well, to tell the truth..." The ideas we forget can be retrieved if we're lucky to have notes and documents. The brand-new ideas can occur accidently while walking the dog, or generated deliberately with the tools from this *Good Thinking Series*, books 3 and 4, and many other resources.

This is just as true for individuals as it is among groups. The ideas we like and think of often are above the line. The ideas that we may know, but not share (even with ourselves), hide in our denial. It's easy to forget ideas. And of course the same idea-generating tools can help individuals come up with ideas on demand when they know how to—and want to.

Junk Drawer

Let's review an experience we've all likely had. I'll assume you have a junk drawer at home. In my many seminar presentations around the world, I have yet to find a modern culture that does not include junk drawers. The junk drawer is a drawer like no others anywhere in the house. It is full of all sorts of odds and ends. And, around the world, we all use it the same way: something is broken, you're hunting for a solution, and you head to the junk drawer. Most of the time, you don't know what you're looking for—other than a solution—but you go to the junk drawer because it's worked before. You open it, scan the objects inside, and *presto!*—some sort of arrangement of the drawer's items jumps out at you as an alternative solution for your problem. You retrieve it and go give it a try. My point is that this happens for all of us, and we've come to rely on it as a method. Given an assortment of seemingly random resources, your brain can make new combinations and end up with a useful alternative that you did not have before.

Part of our work is to get as many good ideas as possible to be part of our conversation by lowering the water line in the diagram above. I'd like a great junk drawer full of optional ideas each time I'm trying to select one to fulfill a need. People can also be like junk drawers. Some are full of lots of options—ideas galore to share. Others have only a few ideas, or the drawer is jammed shut—not open for business.

New Idea Constrainers

It's all well and good to tell someone that they should be a better problem solver, more creative, or a better planner, but there are a factors that limit our creativity, or our attempts to solve problems and plan effectively.

One has to do with our position, our paradigms, how we see things. It seems some people think that the way they see things is the way things are. *"My way or the highway,"* or *"Everyone's entitled to my opinion,"* or, *"Look at these parade marchers: everyone but my son is out of step."*

You've probably been around people who think this way. What happens when you challenge their point of view? They think and act defensively. They likely perceive that you are attacking them, not just their idea. They think of their idea and themselves as one.

Alternatively a person can learn to think that the way they look at things is only a current alternative. We could adopt the attitude that there's always a better way to do or think about something. I can choose to see myself as being on a treasure hunt for better ideas, and not too picky about where these better ideas might come from. I get to decide which ideas I like best. I am not my idea. Another constraint is hunger—hunger for ideas. If people aren't hungry, they won't look.

"It is a universal truth that those who are not dissatisfied will never make any progress. Yet even if one feels dissatisfaction, it must not be diverted into complaining; it must be actively linked to improvement. In this sense, we can say that dissatisfaction is the mother of improvement. There are many examples of waste in the workplace, but not all waste is obvious. It often appears in the guise of useful work. We must see beneath the surface and grasp the essence. Never being content and always looking for ways to make things better are prime prerequisites for uncovering problems."

—Dr. Charles J. Robinson, *Continuous Improvement in Operations: a Systematic Approach to Waste Reduction, Productivity Press,* Portland, Oregon, 1991

When we observe and listen to the dissatisfied person, our challenge is to not take their observations personally. Their feedback may be useful, and our keeping an open mind to the information will most often serve us well.

Another constraint is fear of change. If I can accept that I need new products and services to be competitive, then I need to improve. To improve, I have to change, to start doing something new, and stop doing something old. Ideally I want to change and improve faster than my competitors. I accept I need an effective process to do this.

Eight Ball

There is at least one more constraint: Some people, unfortunately, often pre-judge their own ideas and do not share them with others for a host of social reasons: fear of embarrassment, kidding, seeming stupid—all the usual stuff.

Please help your brain clear itself of old rusty dusty ideas by acknowledging, documenting, and sharing them as they come to your imagination. Do not prejudge. Some of those "bad ideas" are someone else's junk drawer, just what they need to complement what's already in their own junk drawer. They can feed off your ideas and together you can come up with some truly new combinations.

Consider someone playing with that classic toy, the old, fortune-telling Magic Eight Ball. You shake this sphere of truth and—*pop,* up comes an answer. A different answer appeared each time, like a real-time fortune cookie. Have you ever noticed that some people keep shaking the ball until they get the answer they want? "Will I be rich and famous?" "No."..*shake shake...* "Not today."..*shake shake...* "Most certainly." *Ah, we have a winner!* Let the new and possibly different and unexpected ideas be included in your junk drawer. You may find a very good use for then down the road.

New Idea Promoters

The first part of this is easy—reduce or eliminate the constraints. Work hard to lower the water line on the previous iceberg diagram.

In the case of people stuck on their positions, initiating

dialogue is one strategy to develop the opportunity to see things differently. Dialogue is an interactive conversation or experience that generates new knowledge.

This conversation is much improved with the aid of visual and hands-on mark 'em up charts, diagrams, etc., that focus on the current reality to begin with, and then a preferred state. These tools provide the participants a chance to document what's really happening and to question whether the current picture is accurate. These tools then provide the participants a chance to document what they really would prefer.

Finally, the charts and diagrams also provide a neutral place for the participants to look and, importantly, break eye-to-eye contact. People are far more likely to move into an unproductive argument if they're making a lot of eye contact and intent on protecting their position and status. A quick example might be the difference in a traveling couple who is lost with a map and one without a map. Without the map, they just bicker. With the map, they say, "Let's see, where are we?"

In the case of reluctant change participants, it seems that it is in our genes to resist change. Driven by a vision, these steps often take quite a bit of personal courage. People unfamiliar with how to lead innovation do not like change, even though they say they might. People struggle with what to do next. Change, like good ideas, is often only appreciated after it is in place. Successful innovation must be led. Someone in the organization has got to grab the torch and move the troops to a new level of capability.

In the case of hunger, we get motivated when we notice a difference between what we want and what we've got. Scoreboards are helpful here with real, objective numbers reflecting actual performance against goals. And to raise the goals, find and visit another organization that is demonstrating what's possible, i.e. benchmark. These are great learning opportunities for leaders and employees, creating opportunities for them to realize, "Wow, we could do that!"

Ask the Expert

Dr. de Bono, author of *Serious Creativity, Six Thinking Hats, Lateral Thinking,* and many other books about thinking skills defines a productive thinker as:

- confident and competent about their own thinking, not arrogant.
- thinks of themselves as a thinker, not thinking of themselves as intelligent and has all the answers, always right.
- always get better at this skill.
- not always need to be right, can see other people's points of view.
- willing to explore situations, not just defend their point of view.
- willing to look for alternatives and look beyond obvious alternatives.
- can assess priorities and can evaluate alternatives, can make decisions.
- use deliberate creative tools.
- uses Lateral Thinking to generate fresh ideas; not just waiting for an idea, as inspiration or chance has an ability to sit down and generate new ideas; good craftsman, know how to use tools.

Benefits of Collaboration

Productive dialogue provides two significant advantages. One of the perks of effective dialogue is to identify a variety of good alternatives. Another benefit takes advantage of the wonderful principle "People support what they create." It is the combination of good decisions with good support that provides planning team decisions which generate significant business impact.

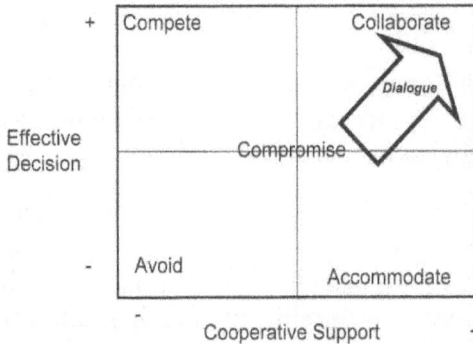

I do want to emphasize the need for both a good decision and good support. A good decision without support is a waste of time. Conversely good support for a bad decision is also a waste of time.

Many leaders think it's sufficient to just clarify their selection of a decision and employees should willingly and skillfully implement the decision. Consider that it's pretty hard for an employee to implement a solution they either don't know much about or do not support.

At the same time, the need for both components can add up to an improved opportunity for success. Imagine a team competing in a multiple event relay race. The next leg of the race asks the team to do the following:

- Run to the beach at the edge of a large lake.
- Pick one of three boats.
- Get across the lake to the next station in the shortest period of time.

There are two issues here: Pick a fast boat (a good decision), and row the boat fast (good support). Don't spend forever making the decision. Make the decision, and then work hard to make the decision a success—row, row, row. Getting out into the middle of the lake and complaining about the choice of the boat is not helpful.

2
Successful Ideation— Fundamental Strategy

Thinking is a Skill

As we learned in *Good Thinking Series,* books 1 and 2, there is a difference between intelligence and thinking. Intelligence is our innate capability, what we're born with. Thinking, on the other hand, is how we learn to use our intelligence, and as such, is a skill. As a skill, like bowling, golfing, cooking, etc., it can be actively improved.

In one comparison, intelligence is the race car and it's finite mechanical capabilities, and thinking is the driver who can learn more and more about how to maximize the utility of the car. In a road racing betting opportunity, would you bet on the car or the driver?

Business Performance Improvement Requires Better Ideas, Better Thinking

Business performance improvement is built on a healthy sequence of improved decisions supported by the decision makers' organizations. Improved decisions come from improved thinking, the ability to solicit, consider, compare, and select good ideas.

```
┌─────────────────────────────────┐
│       Improved Performance      │
└─────────────────────────────────┘
         ↑ Implementation Skills
┌─────────────────────────────────┐
│     Improved Decisions, Support │
└─────────────────────────────────┘
         ↑ Collaboration Skills
┌─────────────────────────────────┐
│         Improved Ideas          │
└─────────────────────────────────┘
         ↑ Idea Generating Skills
┌─────────────────────────────────┐
│        Improved Thinking        │
└─────────────────────────────────┘
```

Effective strategic planning is all about generating lots of good ideas about possible solutions, choosing and confirming the best, and implementing decisions that improve company performance.

Effective scenario planning is all about generating lots of good ideas about possible new products and services that add to company revenues and profit.

In both cases the quality and quantity of good ideas depends on a person or a team's thinking skills.

Better Ideas From Better Thinking

To a layman's view, generating ideas is something that happens. It's a natural phenomenon.

Considering the physiological source of ideas, generating ideas is a neurological phenomenon. Over the past twenty years I have searched for helpful descriptions of this phenomenon. My favorite so far is from David Perkins (*Archimedes' Bathtub: The Art and Logic of Breakthrough Thinking;* Norton & Company, 2000). Perkins' five-step structure describes breakthrough thinking generating new ideas:

22

- **Long Search:** breakthrough thinking characteristically requires a long search
- **Little Apparent Progress:** a typical breakthrough arrives after little or no apparent progress.
- **Precipitating Event:** the typical breakthrough begins with a precipitating event. Sometimes external circumstances cue this moment.
- **Cognitive Snap:** the breakthrough comes rapidly, kind of falling into place, a cognitive snap. Not much time separates the precipitating event from the solution even if details remain to be checked.
- **Transformation:** the breakthrough transforms one's mental or physical world in a generative way.

I find this helpful. It tracks with my experience, individually and as a member of teams.

Without the aid of deliberate thinking skills, working randomly, not knowing any better, I start squinting my eyes and gazing off into space looking for new ideas. It doesn't work too effectively, so it takes quite a while, frustrating me with little progress. Then something happens—bordering on a miracle, depending on the significance of the need for the idea—and the idea snaps into my head like a road sign coming around a bend. Once I have the idea, I'm off to trying it on my need.

For example, I once lost my keys. I did not want to be late to an event so I was under pressure, so my amygdala (emotional decision making area of my brain) kicks in leaving me with emotional thinking and emotional choices: the cat took them, someone moved them (blame blame), I've lost them forever, etc.

So, to practice what I preach, as I could admit that I lost my keys, I sat down to reduce my stress and engage my better thinking. Where in my day's process so far might I have left me keys?. So I imagined my day so far, and long story short, I remembered I took a walk in morning, then chose some clothes to give to the Goodwill store, and had put them in a bag, and *a ha!* The keys were in the pocket of the pants I had worn that morning and put into the bag.

The point of the story is to appreciate that the Perkins model is useful in considering how one organizes their thinking in trying to deliberately come up with useful ideas. In the lost keys case, the precipitating event was choosing to think about the losing of the keys as a process, think it through objectively, and *presto,* the keys were found. Following headless chickens is another, but less useful, method to find one's keys.

The trick is to orchestrate precipitating events on purpose. This can be done by using the techniques and tools presented in the *Good Thinking Series* of books and hundreds of other sources in libraries, the Internet, etc.

Precipitating Events – Why Do They Work?

You might consider that there are three types of thinking:

- **Instinctive:** you decide "automatically"—you pin prick your finger and your hand moves away. Your ride your bike without a paper list of to do's.

- **Emotional:** you decide based on how it feels at the moment. "Oh one more beer is not going to hurt." This type of thinking uses the amygdala of your brain. It seems that when we as people get under stress, for some, anytime they're awake, we default to this level of thinking too often leaving us with decisions we later regret.

- **Intelligent:** you decide based on a comparison of your current options against your goals. This type of thinking engages the prefrontal cortex of your brain where the "executive functioning" takes place. This is where logical thinking occurs. This is the home of the decisions we're glad we made.

Precipitating events work because they engage the prefrontal cortex.

Inside the Box - The Brain's Workings - A Fundamental Primer

My work often presents clients with thinking styles or algorithms (process improvement, creative thinking skills, strategic planning, etc.) in seminars and facilitated meetings which promote or provoke new ideas that clients find valuable. I am, of course, curious if and how these techniques actually work, how a mental exercise can actually develop ideas, on purpose.

I have now twice attended a very helpful conference that has helped me: Hope College's (Holland, MI) Brain and Learning Institute (*www.braininstitute.org*). One speaker, Dr. Marcia Tate (*www.developingmindsinc.com*) provided a very helpful, visual reference of the brain. Place your hands in a praying position. Your hands are about the size of your 3.5 pound brain which is most like a combination of JELL-O and tofu. Your folded hands represent the two halves of your brain. Your thumbs represent the left and right prefrontal cortexes where you do most of your logical thinking and decision making. Your brain includes about 100 billion neurons. Each neuron (cell body) surrounds a nucleus in its center, has a tail called an axon that sends information, and is surrounded by up to six thousand dendrites which receive information. Information is transferred from axons to dendrites via electrochemical impulses that jump the space from axon to dendrite called synapses. Learning grows dendrites—functional MRIs actually see the growth in the nodes on the dendrites as learning progresses.

Brain Friendly Learning

Innovation is fundamentally fast productive learning and implementing. Fast productive learning will happen best when it honors how the brain likes to learn.

What engages axons, and helps grow new dendrites, is great questions. Great questions act as great precipitating events. I call this phenomenon Yenta, after the matchmaker from Fiddler on the Roof. A great question is presented to the brain, the axons become engaged, new information is exchanged electro-chemically between the billions of axons and their dendrites, and Yenta shouts, "Have I got a match for you!" New ideas are formed (cognitive snaps) and new dendrites grow.

Great questions help us grow insights, dendrites, and knowledge. Great questions help us learn. When we ask and answer great questions deliberately, we choose to learn deliberately. The *Good Thinking Series* of books presents many tools—many questions—to promote and provoke learning. Deliberate learning helps us improve and innovate deliberately.

The *Good Thinking Series'* techniques and tools do not tell team members what to think, but *how*. Questions that are answered openly and honestly, with the help of data, in the company of the team members, generate dialogue and learning. This is the opposite of "group think."

Good Thinking Series, books 3 and 4 will help you learn how to deliberately structure "precipitating events" that will more easily lead to "cognitive snaps" and "transformations,"—the very ideas that you're searching for in all areas of work: improvement, innovation, and planning.

3
Introduce Strategic Planning Skills

Strategic planning can be only a time-consuming series of meetings. Treated as a review session of ho-hum initiatives, with little or no preparation, it can be a demoralizing waste of time and effort. Strategic Planning should be a business meeting; no fluff, no guff, no "Kumbaya."

In a sporting comparison it's primarily about a team (soccer, basketball, hockey etc.) deciding they really want to win and work hard to improve their plays and passing until their performance supports their goals. In a non-athletic comparison, we will bring boat building experts together to build a great boat that reflects their collective areas of expertise and contribution. Plan on working till you think the boat will float and you want to get on.

Strategic Planning, done well, is a deep and efficient conversation (dialogue) about an organization's future. Done well it has enormous leverage in guiding an organization to realizing aggressive goals.

Strategic planning meetings usually provide an agenda of predictable questions (Mission, Principles, Scoreboard, etc). This is more convergent than divergent; planning teams often have ten things they'd really like to do over the coming year, but the time and resource to do five or six.

	Tactical	Strategic
Improve **(Convergent)**	Process Improvement Skills	Strategic Planning
	Collaboration Skills	
Innovate **(Divergent)**	Creative Thinking Skills	Scenario Planning

Strategic planning players can include:

- Executive Leaders and their teams.

- Divisional Managers and their teams.

- Project Managers and their teams.

- Supervisors and their teams.

- Anyone who wants to improve their organization's results by developing effective thinking strategies to select and drive an organization's improvement and innovation initiatives.

Effective planning can help you:

- Prepare you and your leadership team to see and act on the future - near term (strategic planning) and long term (scenario planning).

- Make better decisions.

- Build better support for decisions to assure

successful implementation.

- Build team's ability to handle conflict and change.

- Accelerate company improvement and innovation initiatives.

- Turn good thinking into a significant competitive advantage.

Process Considerations

These planning approaches are directed at improving business performance. Improved performance is the result of better decisions, and behaviors associated with the day-to-day communications used in conducting business. Improved decisions and behaviors are the result of improved ideas and insights. And improved ideas and insights are the result of how we think. As stated earlier in this book and other Good Thinking Series books, thinking is an improvable skill. Intelligence is our innate thinking capability, and how we think is how we use this capability.

Planning sessions with senior teams are crucial to a company's success. Effective planning sessions improve the way senior teams think. When facilitated well, a team can come up with preferred alternatives using specific techniques that provoke new ideas while building support for the decisions using specific techniques which promote dialogue. The results of these meetings. great decisions with support to confirm successful implementation, will direct the rest of the organization towards a preferred future.

Taking the Time to Plan vs. "But We're So Busy"

I have learned about planning from four types of planning organizations. The first type does not plan. We all know about companies that are champion fire fighters. Every day is busy busy. Fire fighting is addictive. The busy-ness and activity surrounding fire fighting looks so much like work that many are led astray by a wide variety of new topic-of-the-month initiatives. "Hey, what are you guys working on - a,b,c or d?." " Well, all of them actually, isn't that what you're supposed to...?" Only after the actual results of fire fighting are honestly evaluated does enough frustration occur to move company leaders to take the time and resources to build an internal company wide change capability. Improve and innovate, deliberately. That will keep you plenty busy and productive.

A second type of planning organization goes through the motions of planning, the offsite, the retreat, the three-ring-binders, etc and actually do the work of creating and documenting the plan. But they do not use the plan operationally when they return to their workplace. They too will claim to be too busy.

A third type of planning organization goes through the motions of planning, the offsite, the retreat, the three-ring-binders, etc and actually do the work of creating and documenting the plan. But they believe the plan is more or less secret. They do not share the content of the plan with the organization at large. These leaders believe their employees could not handle either the confidentiality or the complexity of the plan. They protect their employees accordingly.

A fourth and preferred type of planning organization goes through the motions of planning, the offsite, the retreat, the three-ring-binders, etc and actually do the work of creating and documenting the plan. They also engage their employees in the preparation for, the development of, and the sharing of the parts of the plan a particular group of employees need to know in order for them to contribute to the organization. Adults working with adults in an adult manner. This applies to both strategic planning and scenario planning.

Alternate Planning Approaches

While there are certainly more complicated and comprehensive methodologies to support strategic planning (Michigan State's Simplified Strategic Planning process has more than twenty steps, and is presented with 100+ pages of binder text) I have found over the last twenty years that the following documents and process to be what a small to mid-sized company is likely to take the time to develop and use. A more comprehensive systems approach, supported by fewer people, will work against the goal of aligning a whole organization.

Strategic Planning vs. Annual Planning

Strategic planning provides a macro multi-year view of where you want to go, and broadly how. Annual planning provides a focused micro single-year view of how you will organize and exercise the resources necessary to achieve your strategic plan

Annual Planning Process

1. Determine what your sales are likely to be in the coming year.

2. Figure out what it's going to cost to produce these sales and how much cash you can expect to generate as a result.

3. Decide what you want to do with the cash.

4. Choose your bonus goals for the year.

Annual Planning Components

1. Income statement.
2. Balance sheet.
3. Cash-flow analysis.
4. Sales and marketing plan.
5. Capital plan.
6. Inventory plan.
7. Organization charts.
8. Compensation plan.

There is an excellent Introduction to annual planning in chapters 8 and 9 of Jack Stack's *The Great Game of Business* (1992, New York: Currency Paperback).

Strategic Planning Components

Strategic Planning most often includes the following documents which provide the listed types of information.

1. **Mission:** "Who we are, what we do;" ultimate intent of organization; no time constraint.

2. **Principles:** "How we work together;" rules about how we treat ourselves, each other, and our community. How we think and behave to keep ourselves on track.

3. **Scoreboard:** "Success as measured by..." tactical or strategic; measurable performance expectations.

4. **Vision:** "Where we want to be;" a long view, 3-5 years, of what must be accomplished to support the Purpose.

5. **Business Environment:** "Playing field; even and uneven;" listing of internal and external promoting and restraining forces that will affect business performance.

6. **Objectives:** "What to do next;" specific milestones of what must be accomplished in the next year to support the Vision. Usually three to five are useful.

7. **Strategies:** "How to" accomplish Objectives while considering business environment requirements. Usually three to five per Objective are useful.

8. **Action Plans:** "To do assignments;" quarterly, prioritized action steps necessary to support the Objectives and Strategies. Usually three to five per Strategy are useful.

9. **Plan Implementation Considerations:** Proliferation plans, announcements plan, budget plan, barriers.

10. **Plan Monitoring Considerations:** Criteria and plan to monitor your progress, to a preferred set of decisions, and when effectively led and implemented, delivers the organization success.

Effective strategic planning can be thought of as a great sequence of questions which helps lead an organization to a preferred set of decisions when effectively led and implemented delivers organization success. If we only review what has happened, we need not be creative. But if we plan to evaluate our progress and select new responses and approaches, we need to be creative where business creativity is the deliberate ability to generate additional useful alternatives, tactical and strategic.

Think of these documents as a hierarchy of intent, from the biggest ideas all the way down to the entries in your daily planner. The purpose of specific titles for each document/technique/question is to allow each planning team member and employee use the terms the same way. Select terms that would best fit in your culture. Planning is an iterative process meaning as we move into exercises and documents later in a session, and learn something that would affect a previous document, we go back and improve it. We want all the documents to be optimized together s a whole.

One alternate strategic planning process would have an expert/facilitator come to your organization, conduct multiple interviews, go back to their office, write your plan, and deliver it to your senior team. Very easy for the senior team, terrible for either engaging the players or building support. Another would have a large group of senior team with management meet for multiple sessions (20+ I kid you not), bore and demoralize the attendees and occasionally not even end up with a plan to implement. Nice to know you have choices.

Systems Thinking

One model of thinking which helps leaders to get their arms around planning in an organization is "a system." Think of a system as an interdependent collection of components and processes. A garden is a helpful example of a system. The components include soil, water, nutrients, sun, plants, weeds, etc. Some gardens look great, some don't. The gardens that are a pleasure to view and walk through are the result of a person who knows how their group of variables can be best developed, coordinated and maintained. Without the knowledge, skill, and initiative of how to coordinate the variables, a garden is just another weed patch.

Organizations are complicated systems which include thousands of variables and processes which together generate the results and successes of an organization. Led well they are pleasurable places to work.

Strategic Plan Format – Example # 1 - (abbreviated)

To assist the planning team in preparing to contribute to the same document during the planning process, we will also want to identify some parameters for each of the documents listed below.

1. Definition: what information should this document provide?
2. Intended Audience: for whom is this document intended?
3. Intended Utility: how will this document and its content be used?
4. Criteria Describing an Excellent Example: what criteria must the document satisfy?

ABC Enterprises

1. Mission:

- *Definition:* "who we are, what we do;" ultimate intent of organization; no time constraint.
- *Audience:* all employees, leaders, customers, investors, vendors, community.
- *Utility:* inform audience what organization is all about.
- *Criteria:* short, easy to remember.

Example:

- Provide excellent products and services nationwide.

- Help private and public clients in the area of *xyz*.

2. Principles:

- *Definition:* "how we work together;" rules about how we treat ourselves, each other, and our community. How we think and behave to keep ourselves on track.
- *Audience:* all employees, leaders, customers, investors, vendors, community.
- Utility: inform audience about our ground rules and behavior standards. Provide a reference point for tough or tempting times when leaders and employees may be tempted to violate better thinking and behavior.
- Criteria: address specific issues which may be potential problems for the organization.

Examples:

- Integrity. Commitment to customers.
- Fair. Helping Others.

3.Scoreboard:

- *Definition:* "success as measured by...;" tactical or strategic; measurable performance expectations.
- *Audience:* all employees, leaders, vendors
- *Utility:* provide real-time, accurate feedback to organization about its current performance,
- *Criteria:* clear list of components and metrics:

Example:

- Quality
    - complaints on fewer than 5% orders
    - measurable improvement on 75% of our processes
- Cost
    - operating at or below operating expense plans
    - Current Programs
    - supporting 15 programs as outlined in 2010 strategic plan
- New Programs
    - supporting 2 new programs per half year as outlined in 2010 strategic plan
- Employee Morale
    - employee turnover less than 10% per year

4. Vision:

- *Definition:* "where we want to be;" a long view, 3-5 years, of what must be accomplished to support the Purpose.
- *Audience:* all employees, leaders, customers, investors, vendors
- *Utility:* inform audience about long range goals. Provides a clear target that tends to pull the whole organization in one direction.
- *Criteria:* clear list of objectives that inspire the audience.

Example:

- Build a business in the area of xyz which generates $xyz by January 20XX

- Be and be perceived as the premier company in the area of xyz by January 20XX

5. Business Environment:

- *Definition:* "playing field; even and uneven;" listing of ranked internal and external forces that promote or restrain the organizations efforts for success.

- *Audience:* all leaders

- *Utility:* Focus subsequent objectives, strategies, and actions. Write objectives, strategies, and actions that maintain the high ranking promoting forces, and reduce or eliminate the high ranking restraining forces.

- *Criteria:* short, ranked list for each of the four areas: internal promoting, internal restraining, external promoting, external restraining.

Example

Internal Promoting	Internal Restraining
1. strong staff	1. billable hours
2. firm commitment	2. diverse agendas
3. helpful partners	
4. talent pool	

External Promoting	External Restraining
1. limited competition	1. employment rate
2. market interest	2. e business buzz
3. referring clients	3. dispersion of client location
4. client loyalty	

6. Objectives; 7. Strategies; 8. Actions:

- *Objective definition:* "what to do next;" specific milestones of what must be accomplished in the next year to support the Vision. Usually three to five are useful.

- *Strategy definition:* "how to" accomplish Objectives while considering business environment requirements. Usually three to five per Objective are useful.

- *Action Plans definition:* "to do assignments;" quarterly, prioritized action steps necessary to support the Objectives and Strategies. Usually three to five per Strategy are useful.

- *Audience:* all employees, leaders

- *Utility:* Inform audience of expectations at three levels

- *Criteria:* clear expectations with metrics to be accomplished over the next 12 months.

Examples:

1. Objective: Build a network which generates 60% billings by January, 20XX
    1a. Strategy: Identify and establish a contact program for two referral sources
        1a1. Action Plan: AB Attend Joint seminars; one per quarter;$3,000
        1a2. Action Plan: CD complete Mailing list contacts; update monthly: $200
        1a3. Action Plan: MJ attend referral source sponsored programs; one per quarter; $2500
    1b. Identify 5-10 clients or potential clients for the contact program.
        1b1. LK establish and calendar a plan for quarterly contact.(Lunches, breakfasts, entertainment) $0
        1b2. GI conduct 3 off-the-clock visits to client location; $150

2. Bring in one new significant established client (> $xyz annual billing) and one new emerging growth client (> $xyz annual billing) every year.

    2b. Identify four target clients for 20XX.

    2b1. YG form target "hunting" teams.$300

    2b2. DO establish and implement an action plan $0

9. Plan Implementation Considerations:

- *Definition:* proliferation plans, announcements plan, budget plan, barriers.

- *Audience:* all leaders

- *Utility:* help leaders address plan implementation speed bumps and road blocks.

- *Criteria:* comprehensive list of tasks that must be accomplished to support the successful implementation of the plan.

Example:

- Control printing and distribution of plan copies

- Meet with appropriate teams to explain plan and answer questions

- Listen for rumors and bring to leadership team to develop consistent response to be then shared by all leaders.

- Make sure old versions of plans are destroyed.

10. Plan Monitoring Considerations: criteria and plan to monitor your progress

- *Definition:* criteria and plan to monitor your progress

- *Audience:* all leaders
- *Utility:* Provide to do list and schedule of meetings that will have leadership team review plan progress and identify any work necessary to support plan.
- *Criteria:* schedule and agenda of review meetings

Example:

- Leadership will meet the first Tuesday of even months for two hours (9-11AM) to review strategic plan.

Additional Considerations for Strategic Planning

While an organization's fellow leaders and employees can facilitate problem solving and creative thinking skills sessions well, I do not recommend they facilitate strategic planning sessions. Planning participants often include some forceful egos who need to be managed to allow the group to have group-wide dialogue, not just a conversation between a few members of the leadership team. Strategic planning sessions need a meeting coach from outside the organization.

Good planning facilitators, experienced with the process and techniques of successful facilitation and respected by the audience, can help senior teams significantly. Poor facilitators have an equally negative effect Good planning facilitators have extra training in project management, group process, and effective meeting process techniques.

I encourage you to identify someone who has at least one of the following six of the following eight skills and is trainable in the other three:

- Knows how to help others learn.
- Likes working to generate data to substantiate decisions.
- Able to work with customers and suppliers.
- Can go toe-to-toe with employees at all levels.
- Focuses the team's process.
- Assists leader in breaking down tasks.
- Works with team leader between meetings to plan upcoming meetings.
- Prepares and presents training.
- Helps teams prepare presentations.

The consulting firm BlessingWhite looks for individuals who possess both expertise and superior presentation skills, because an outstanding facilitator will contribute significantly to the success of any program. Here is a representative list of the criteria they use to select their facilitators.

Qualities:

- Interested in self-development and inspiring others to change and grow.
- Likes working with ideas and quickly grasps new ones.
- Is "quick on his/her feet;" manages the environment and dynamics of a group by handling ambiguity, showing flexibility, and reacting appropriately to unanticipated responses or issues.
- Listens closely and articulates ideas; is a good communicator.

- Has the right balance of facilitation/presentation skills and relevant work/life experience.
- Creates and maintains strong partnerships with others.
- Acts as both facilitator and consultant.
- Has enthusiasm for what he/she is doing.
- Embraces company's mission, values, and basic beliefs.

A quick summary would encourage you to find someone your planning team can learn with. I have heard about planning experts who bore teams to death. I have heard about planning facilitators who are forceful about their process but irritate the planning members.

And I've heard about planning facilitators who absolutely make a difference for the planning sessions; more work in less time, more commitment and more fun. Find a facilitator that fits your planning team; there needs to be a positive chemistry so good work can be accomplished.

2. Planning Team Preparation – Communication Skills

Effective planning meetings will include a series of interactive table exercises intended to both identify preferred decisions and develop support necessary to successfully implement the decisions. Planning teams end each exercise with a confirmed or revised version of a component of their plan. Planning teams develop the plan on a series of flip charts, their work bench, as we move through the exercises. In building the organization's plan, they may not complete every exercise, and they may do some exercisers not included in their meeting agenda.

The strategic planning meeting is being held to allow

each team member "to be heard." This meeting should be very interactive. Plan to take full advantage of the principle "people support what they create." An understanding of the collaboration principles outlined in *Good Thinking Series* Book 2, *Collaborate,* will very much enhance the efficiency and effectiveness of the meeting.

Business performance improvement depends on making AND supporting better decisions. Decisions can be made by either one person or a team. The vast majority of decisions are implemented by teams. To maximize the impact of these decisions, we want to maximize the contribution each team member is willing and able to make in helping to implement the decision. We can do this by training and expecting team members to work as a team to build decisions each member wants to support. Dialogue is one effective strategy to both build great decisions AND develop great support.

Effective collaboration has two tasks and needs. One is to ask the team to identify the best alternative. Good meetings actively promote identifying and prioritizing best choices often hiding in a wide variety of strongly-held personal opinions. Sometimes it's adequate to just brainstorm and select. But at other times teams need to get past the "politically correct" speed bumps and get the water cooler issues on the table so they too can be considered. And still other times, the best ideas haven't been discovered yet.

A second component is to deliberately build support for the team's selections by organizing the dialogue to promote participant contribution and buy-in. Here we want to take advantage of the wonderful principle that people support what they create. When people are included in the identification, comparison, and selection of alternatives, most often a very good solution emerges which everyone can support.

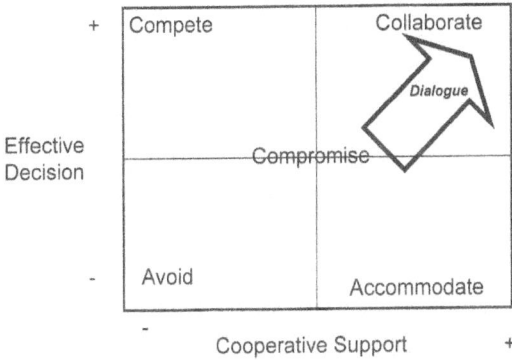

Adapted from Thomas-Kilmann model

It is this combination of both better decisions and better support that provides team decisions which generate significant business impact.

Dealing with Conflict

People being people, generating effective dialogue to promote the necessary learning is sometimes difficult. At two ends of the participant behavior scale are 1. a painfully quiet restricted conversation, and 2. a loud competition of interpersonal challenges. We're targeting productive dialogue where each member gets heard and the team builds decisions each member supports.

Often these planning sessions and similar meetings can get derailed. Somewhere along the way we discover that others don't always see things the same way we do. We seem to be in conflict. Conflict is in large part the emotional reaction we experience when we think a particular way. Sometimes conflict is disabling, preventing future progress. Sometimes conflict is laughable upon discovering a misunderstanding.

"Conflict is definitely a growth industry."

—Roger Fisher, *Harvard Negotiation Project and Getting to Yes*

Effective planning teams learn how to think and behave in ways that help them move past conflict.

As mentioned a number of times in earlier articles, good company performance comes from good decisions and behaviors, which come from good ideas which come from good thinking If I want to improve my company's performance, what's the best way to think about this?." In this case how a team thinks about conflict has a significant effect on the results of a meeting.

A helpful way to think while planning as a team:

- **Point of View:** a person's particular way of looking at things, their paradigm, their position. Our paradigms are the result of the interaction of our conditioned perceptual skills and reinforced experiences.

- **Conflict:** discovery of different points of view.

- **Challenge:** an impersonal request to consider an alternative point of view.

- **Fallibility:** acceptance of fallibility celebrates you're not done with who you can become.

- **Shared Understanding:** an improved understanding of the breadth and depth of an issue as a result of dialogue.

- **Equifinality:** the notion that there is not only one way to do something, but rather a number of ways which, successfully supported, will generate an acceptable result. Our goal is to pick a good one, and deliberately make it a success.

- **Collaboration:** Collaborating involves an attempt to work all members of a team to find an alternative that meets all sets of concerns. It means digging into an issue to identify the underlying concerns of the team members and to find and alternative that meets all sets of concerns. Collaborating might take the form of exploring a disagreement to learn from each other's insights, concluding to resolve some condition which would otherwise have them competing for resources, or confronting and trying to find a creative solution to an interpersonal problem.

3. Planning Team Preparation – Prework

To contribute to the planning meeting participants will want to prepare and firm up their own hopes and strategies for what they believe their organization can accomplish. The planning team will work to focus on data based positions vs. strong opinions. If a participant has a project which needs to be considered by the team, the participant should have their facts and data to substantiate their point of view. Participants should consider any work before this meeting that would promote their causes at this meeting.

Participants will benefit from spending time working through any planning preparation documents and their exercises alongside their copy of the organization's current plan. The better participants are prepared to present and discuss the important factors that contribute to their plan, the better plan they will build, and the better support they will develop as a team for their plan. No participants in a planning session should plan to audit the session.

Pre-work can include any study that helps you develop effective documents that each planning member wants to support.

Regarding content, participants can only sing the songs they know. I would encourage participants in the days before they meet to expand their repertoire of great ideas by nosing around in magazines, books, remarkable thinkers heads (young and old), museums, client sites, web sites, etc etc hunting for trends that they think their company can identify and take advantage of. This is an important step. Participants should plan on surprising their team with the breadth and quality of their ideas. Heroes are made in overtime.

Find time to read about or actually visit with "remarkable thinkers" — those individuals who may most often be off your radar screen but who are bit obsessed with your topic of interest and have thought way out there. They can really stretch what you may have to offer in your session.

Best case participants come prepared with good data, an open mind, and an attitude that will contribute to their organization's success. Best case participants arrive loaded with new knowledge about the products and processes of their own company, their customers, and their competitors.

Attendees

The participants to the planning session should represent the functions of an organization, the components of the company's system: sales, marketing, service, human resources, etc. I prefer for there to be only one representative to each department to keep the size of the planning team to less than twelve.

Interviews

I much prefer to meet with Planning Team members one-on-one about a week or two before a planning session to discuss each person's perceptions of the opportunities and barriers their team needs to consider in the group meetings. In these meetings I ask the following questions:

1. What is your business?
2. What are your business's goals and measurements of success?
3. Who are the winner/loser businesses that are your competitors?
4. How should your business differentiate itself from its competitors?
5. What are the top five opportunities do you see for your business?
6. What are the top five barriers to success do you see for your business?
7. What is your role in your business?
8. How do you measure your success and how do you like to be rewarded?
9. How would you describe your executive team regarding leadership, decision making, and getting things done?

I distribute this list before the interviews and ask that each person prepare their responses. Ideally each Planning Team member develops their own version, even if just outlined, of the organizations whole plan. Think big, think about the whole organization and how the different departments and their initiatives must work together.

The information from these interviews is completely confidential. Planning team members will choose if and when they want any of their information shared with the team. At the same time I am much better prepared to develop and present exercises to maximize the chance that the Planning Team will talk about the most important issues during the planning session.

Session Format - What to Expect

Participants sit at team tables facing a series of flip charts where the ideas for each agenda/step are placed as the participants generate them. We treat the series of flip charts as a whole. If we get down the road and think of a good idea to include in an earlier step, we do so. Participants are focused on each step, engaged in idea generation and consideration, and up on their feet often to present ideas and reconfigure the flip charts.

At the end of the session you will leave with the roll of completed flip charts which will most likely be collated back in your office by administrative staff.

Preparing for Planning Sessions – Helpful Tool: Key Decision Charts

Strategic Planning is fundamentally an appropriate sequence of questions that answered outlines substantive content and support for initiatives that will guide an organization for months and years to come.

It is best if each planning team member is fully aware of the decisions and support they need for the plan to include to allow them to complete their own functional initiatives. This section about Key Decision Charts will describe one way for planning team members to identify these decisions and support that they need addressed during a strategic planning session to allow them to complete their own team's responsibilities.

Developing Key Decision Charts

Each planning team member develops a Key Decisions Chart for themselves a few weeks before the planning session. Their chart outlines their own department's key decisions that need to be made within three time periods: Year 1, Years 2-3, and Years 4-5.

This can be developed on a flip chart or in an Excel spread sheet. The sheet has three columns (time periods) and five rows (five key decisions/support, one per row). Each of the fifteen cells would list the following information:

1. Topic:

    a. Decision to be made?

    b. Do I have the data to make the decision?

    c. Do I have the support to implement the decision?

    Chart format:

KEY DECISIONS CHART		Name - Date
Year 1	Years 2 - 3	Years 4 - 5
1. Topic 1a. Decision to be made: 1b. Do I have the **data** to make the decision? 1c. Do I have the **support** to implement the decision? include up to 5 key decisions per column	same format as column 1 considering years 2-3	same format as column 1 considering years 4-5

It is also helpful to assign a colored dot alongside the description of each topic's data and support listings to indicate the author's level of comfort with this task.

- green = on track
- yellow = needs some attention, speed bumps present

- red = roadblocks present

Chart example for one of the cells:

KEY DECISIONS CHART - EXAMPLE		Name - Date
Year 1	Years 2 - 3	Years 4 - 5
1.Site Consolidation 1a. Should we consolidate the operations currently at sites X and Y? Yellow dot: 1b. (data) I need to know the financial implications across all the sites of completing this move. I need to consider the incoming demographics for the next 10 years. Red dot: 1c. (support) I need know if the leaders of sites X and Y would support this move.	same format as column 1 considering years 2-3	same format as column 1 considering years 4-5

This chart boils down to being a department's target list for its own functional strategic plan. It's value comes from both the preparation by the functional leader and the valuable dialogue among other functional leaders, the whole planning team, during the presentations.

Meet to Identify Target Decisions

The meeting described here takes place a few weeks before a planning session. This is a collaborative dialogue session. Each planning team member presents their chart to the planning team. The yellow and red dots provide some focus for the presentation "Here's where I'm in need regarding a topic/decision/support – who can help me with recommended contacts, approaches, resources, etc?"

As an example of a similar kind of meeting, imagine a group is assembling to build a sail boat. The participants represent expertise in sail making, hull building, anchor placement, cabin arrangements, etc. As one person talks about their needs, the others, representing other components of the boat's building, know plenty about how the presenter's issues and questions affect their area of responsibility. Collaborative planning team members also respect that each presenter needs to win for the boat to be a success. This deep dialogue provides the opportunity to identify and coordinate all the boat's interdependent components. Woe be to the crew that assumes other members know what they need.

Importantly the purpose of the presentation is not to look good. This is a meeting to help the team recognize where they need to do some work to improve their ability to write a more effective strategic plan. Honest presentation and feedback is crucial.

Monitor During the Planning Session

During the planning session the Key Decision Chart is like a shopping list for each of the planning team members. Each needs to make sure the new Strategic Plan supports them so they can complete the tasks outlined on their Key Decision Chart while they help others do the same.

4. Work Area Set Up

I prefer large rooms (1,500 square feet) with windows and lots of wall space. I like moveable smaller tables (4-6 people per table) with comfortable chairs.

I recommend planning teams sit at team tables facing a series of flip charts posted on a wall where the ideas (written on Post Its) for each planning step are placed as you generate them.

This meeting is a very interactive, hands-on, hard-work session. Participants work at team tables, writing their ideas on Post Its, moving to flip charts, and presenting their results to small and large groups. Participants are focused on each step, one-at-a-time, engaged in idea generation and consideration, and up on their feet often to present ideas and reconfigure the flip charts.

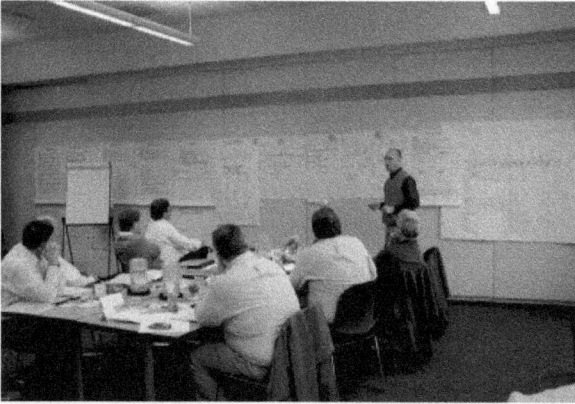

This photo shows one group reviewing their work; no projector/screen. Flip Charts on wall are sequenced in the 1-10 steps of the planning process. Room has good light (windows to speaker's left). Tables set to allow participants to view presenter without having to turn around. Great wall space. Great move around space.

Materials include markers for flip charts and Post Its, Post Its, flip chart stand and paper, and masking tape (blue if possible) to tape flip charts up. Do not use "permanent" markers, they can bleed through flip charts and mark walls.

At the end of the session clients have a roll of completed flip charts which will most likely be collated by their administrative staff.

5. Prepare to Document and Discuss Ideas – Brainstorming with Post Its

I have been accused of owning plenty of 3M stock – I really like to use Post its. I could be their poster child. The reason, I have come to think of Post Its as the currency of dialogue. This low technology communication tool, when used appropriately, can very much not only manage the gathering and presentation of valuable ideas, it can also promote the dialogue necessary to build collaboration, to build good decisions and good buy in.

Any successful ideation and discussion process must address the social pressures often present in groups when they are asked to perform. Some examples of the factors to consider:

Some participants:

- Don't want to go first.
- Always want to go first.
- Don't want to talk much.
- Always talk and fill in any silence gap.
- Have no agenda.
- Have their own agenda.
- Etc.

So, to my experience and eye, it seems the following simple process handles most of these issues quite well.

Step 1: Clarify which document you are working on

Clarify title and: a) audience, b) utility, and c) criteria.

Step 2: Develop Ideas for the document's content

First have team members silently write their alternatives one idea per Post It. It is often helpful to brainstorm a few ideas as a large group to calibrate the group to the process and possible ideas. Give team members about five minutes to work silently on their own. Quotas are helpful, say at least five ideas/Post Its per person.

Step 3: Present and Discuss Ideas

In an orderly manner, have each member of the team, sitting around a table or standing facing a flip chart posted on the wall, share their ideas one-at-a-time as they place their entries on the flip chart. If a team member has no new entries, they may pass. If they think of new ones, they can get back into the sequence when their turn comes in the next go-round.

Step 4: Group Ideas and rank if useful - silently

The option to group the Post its (Affinity Diagram) silently takes away any influence a more-verbal member of the participants may want to exert. Once the Post Its are grouped, nod to confirm everyone's ok with the arrangement, then discuss and post the titles to the groups. If helpful, have the team select the ideas that have the highest impact on the business.

Step 5: Confirm the resulting document is good enough to move on knowing that you can change it as you progress through subsequent document exercises.

The keys to the success of this approach is to give people time to do their work (five minutes alone quietly) without pressure, and then process to give each participant the chance to be heard (one idea at a time, one person at a time, till all the ideas are posted) without having to step forward assertively. The facilitator trick here is to structure the team's work so the team gets what it wants: good ideas with good support.

Note: Do not work on documents, especially during the first trial, to make them perfect. Thirty minutes ought to build a pretty good start for a Mission Statement. You do not need three days in a cottage in the English countryside to do this work.

Planning is an iterative process meaning as we move into exercises and documents later in a session, and learn something that would affect a previous document, we go back and improve it. We want all the documents to be optimized as a whole.

4

Practice Strategic Planning Skills

The exercise steps listed below include those I most often facilitate in a client strategic planning session.

I prepare the planning room by posting the entire planning process on flip charts, one step per chart, along a long wall in the planning room.

Depending on the client, I will ask some of the following questions to warm up a planning team.

Stretching Exercises - Planning Team Mental Warm Up

1. Regarding your major competitors, what are their plans for you? How do you show up on their strategic and/or tactical plans?

2. If your funding genie could buy you three things (capability, facilities, frame of mind, anything) what would you ask for?

3. What are your employees likely saying about the performance of this planning team? Are there some popular topics? What grade would your employees give this planning team for successful implementation of strategic action items? Is there a

range of opinions? Are these views affecting your company's performance?

4. What are you most proud of about working at your company?

5. You have just won the lottery and have chosen to spend one more day at your company. What would you do if you wanted to provide the highest positive impact?

6. If your organization was purchased in a friendly takeover, and all of you gladly accepted very generous golden parachutes and membership in the board of directors, what characteristics would you establish for the new leadership team?

7. What is one thing this planning team has troubling thinking about? What is the undiscussable topic that goes undiscussed? What do the water coolers hear that this team doesn't talk about?

8. What is the most controversial topic we should deal with this week?

9. What is one question you really want to ask this team?

10. What three things do you spend most of your time on at work?

11. What is one thing you really like about working with this team?

12. What is the biggest hole you have in your product/service offerings?

13. If your spouse had an opportunity to advise this team about its work, what would they recommend?

14. What are the top three things that restrain you from achieving the initiatives outlined in your planning documents?

15. What decisions do you want this team to tackle this week to help you work to achieve the initiatives outlined in your planning documents?

Exercise 1 Mission

"Who we are, what we do;" ultimate intent of organization; no time constraint. Some organizations like to include the names of major players (customers, employees, etc.).

You might consider this your "elevator speech," what you would say to introduce yourself in less than a minute.

Exercise Process:

As a team facing a flip chart, at the top of the flip chart:

1. Document <u>audience</u> of this document.
2. Document <u>purpose</u> of this document.
3. Document <u>criteria</u> of this document.

Alone:

4. Writing one idea per Post-It note, silently brainstorm your ideas.

As a team facing a flip chart:

5. Place your entries on the flip chart one idea at a time, one person at a time.
6. Discuss and organize the entries into groups.

7. Identify the titles to the groups.

8. Write a paragraph or phrase that includes the chart's major ideas.

Mission - Example Criteria:

(from (C/P), James C. Collins, and Jerry I. Porras, (1996); "Building Your Company's Vision;" Harvard Business Review September-October 1996, pp. 65-77)

- Reason for being....reflects people's idealistic motivations for doing the company's work." (C/P p.68).

- "It doesn't just describe the organization's output or target customers; it captures the soul of the organization" (C/P p.68).

- "Makes a contribution to customers success" (C/P p.70).

- Not "maximize shareholder wealth" (C/P p.70).

- Tested with the "Random Corporate Serial Killer game;" what would be lost if the company ceased to exist? (C/P p.70, 71).

- Passes the "So what?" test.

Examples of Organizational Missions:

Rotary International 2007-2010

The mission of Rotary International, a worldwide association of Rotary clubs, is to provide service to others, promote high ethical standards, and advance world understanding, goodwill, and peace through its fellowship of business, professional, and community leaders.

Note: Rotary International is the world's first

service club organization, with more than 1.2 million members in 33,000 clubs worldwide. Rotary club members are volunteers who work locally, regionally, and internationally to combat hunger, improve health and sanitation, provide education and job training, promote peace, and eradicate polio under the motto Service Above Self (www.rotary.org).

Apple

Apple is committed to bring the best personal computing products and support to students, educators, designers, scientists, engineers, businesspersons, and consumers in over 140 countries around the world. (page 72, *The Mission Book,* Jeffrey Abrahams)

Avis Rent a Car

To ensure a stress-free rental experience by providing safe, dependable vehicles and special services designed to win the customer's loyalty. (page 79, *The Mission Book,* Jeffrey Abrahams)

Chase Manhattan Corporation

We provide financial services that contribute to the success of individuals, businesses, communities, and countries around the world. By creating solutions for our customers, opportunities for our employees, and superior returns for our shareholders, we help to achieve our goals. (page 112, The Mission Book, Jeffrey Abrahams)

Coca Cola

We exist to create value for our shareholders on a

long-term basis. We refresh the world. We do this by developing superior beverage products that create value for our company, our bottling partners, and our customers. (page 132, *The Mission Book*, Jeffrey Abrahams).

Exercise 2: Principles

"How we work together, rules about how we treat ourselves, each other, and our community; how we think and behave at our best."

I like to think of this as a description of how we think and behave to keep ourselves on track.

Exercise Process:

As a team facing a flip chart, at the top of the flip chart:

1. Document <u>audience</u> of this document.

2. Document <u>purpose</u> of this document.

3. Document <u>criteria</u> of this document.

Alone:

4. Writing one idea per Post-It note, silently brainstorm your ideas.

As a team facing a flip chart:

5. Place your entries on the flip chart one idea at a time, one person at a time.

6. Discuss and organize the entries into groups.

7. Identify the titles to the groups.

8. Write a paragraph or phrase that includes the chart's major ideas.

Principles – Example Considerations:

- "What we stand for, why we exist....Enduring character of an organization - a consistent identity that transcends product or market life cycles, technological breakthroughs, management fads, and individual leaders."..."the glue that holds an organization together as it grows, decentralizes, diversifies, expands globally, and develops workplace diversity (C/P p.66)...role of core ideology is to guide and inspire, not differentiate. (C/P p.70) Collins & Porras.

- ."..the essential and enduring tenants of an organization. A small set of timeless principles,...require no external justification. Cannot be created, only discovered." (C/P p. 71).

- "We would have them even if they became a competitive disadvantage in certain situations." A small set of timeless principles (C/P p.66).

- "Companies tend to have only a few core values, usually between three and five." (C/P p.67).

- "Not to be confused with operating practices, business strategies, or cultural norms (which should be open to change)."(C/P p.67).

- "If the circumstances changed and penalized us for hold this core value, would we still keep it? If you can't honestly answer yes, then the value is not core and should be dropped from consideration." (C/P p.67)

(C/P), James C. Collins, and Jerry I. Porras, (1996); "Building Your Company's Vision;" Harvard Business Review September-October 1996, pp. 65-77.

Example - Rotary International 2007-2010

Conduct only activities that are:

1. the TRUTH.
2. FAIR to all concerned.
3. will it build GOODWILL and BETTER FRIENDSHIPS.
4. will it be BENEFICIAL to all concerned.

Exercise 2 – Values Example

Some organizations like to separate values and principles. Values can be thought of as the things we hold most dear. Principles can be thought of as how we think and behave to honor and preserve the values.

Use the same process stated above for Principles.

Example - Rotary International 2007-2010

Rotary's core values represent the guiding principles of the organization's culture, including what guides members' priorities and actions within the organization. Values are an increasingly important component in strategic planning because they drive the intent and direction of the organization's leadership.

- **Service:** We believe that our service activities and programs bring about greater world understanding and peace. Service is a major element of our mission. Through the plans and actions of individual clubs, we create a culture of service throughout our organization that provides unparalleled satisfaction for those who serve.

- **Fellowship:** We believe that individual efforts focus on individual needs, but combined efforts serve humanity. The power of combined efforts knows no limitation, multiplies resources, and broadens our lives and perspectives. Fellowship leads to tolerance and transcends racial, national, and other boundaries.

- **Diversity:** We believe Rotary unifies all people internationally behind the ideal of service. We encourage diversity of vocations within our membership and in our activities and service work. A club that reflects its business and professional community is a club with a key to its future.

- **Integrity:** We are committed to and expect accountability from our leaders and fellow members, both in the results of our efforts and in the processes we use to accomplish our goals. We adhere to high ethical and professional standards in our work and personal relationships. We are fair and respectful in our interactions, and we conscientiously steward the resources entrusted to us.

- **Leadership:** We are a global fellowship of individuals who are leaders in their fields of endeavor. We believe in the importance of leadership development and in leadership as a quality of our members. As Rotarians, we are leaders in implementing our core values.

Exercise 3: Scoreboard

"Success as measured by...," tactical or strategic; measurable performance expectations.

Your organization's scoreboard can be thought of as

your work and plan's dashboard. How can you measure your key driving factors to confirm you're on track to achieve your vision, objectives, etc.

Your scoreboard will list what you talk about/measure when you ask among yourselves as leaders, "How are things going?"

Exercise Process:

As a team facing a flip chart, at the top of the flip chart:

1. Document <u>audience</u> of this document.

2. Document <u>purpose</u> of this document.

3. Document <u>criteria</u> of this document.

Alone:

4. Writing one idea per Post-It note, silently brainstorm your ideas.

As a team facing a flip chart:

5. Place your entries on the flip chart one idea at a time, one person at a time.

6. Discuss and organize the entries into groups.

7. Identify the titles to the groups.

Example

- Quality
  - complaints on fewer than 5% orders
  - measurable improvement on 75% of our processes

- Cost
  - operating at or below operating expense plans
- Current Programs
  - supporting fifteen programs as outlined in 2001 strategic plan
- New Programs
  - supporting two new programs per half year as outlined in 2001 strategic plan
- Employee Morale
  - employee turnover less than 10% per year

A "Balanced Scorecard" includes both leading and lagging measurables.

Balanced Scorecard:

- Leading
  - learning and growth
  - internal business processes
  - proactive customer support
- Lagging
  - financial

Rotary International 2007-2010

Example: (my outline, I did not find one for Rotary International)

- **Polio:** % remaining cases.
- **Public Image:** Survey results.
  - **Club Growth:** Number of new clubs in current and new areas.

- **Membership:** Number of new members in current and new areas.

- **Vocational Service Support:** Number of students supported by clubs.

- **Leadership Development:** Number of attendees in current and new leadership classes and roles.

Exercise 4: Vision

"Where we want to be;" a long view, 1-3 years, of what must be accomplished to support the Purpose.

Exercise Process:

As a team facing a flip chart, at the top of the flip chart:

1. Document <u>audience</u> of this document.

2. Document <u>purpose</u> of this document.

3. Document <u>criteria</u> of this document.

4. Imagine a very positive picture of your organization from a time one to three years from now.

Alone:

5. Brainstorm your ideas. One idea per Post It. Include a number of projects, accomplishments, major changes, etc. Let your imaginations run.

As a team facing a flip chart

6. Meet at a flip chart and present your ideas, one at a time as we have before. Add new ideas as they come up in your conversation.

7. Using flip charts sheet, write your stories in the format of prestigious publication such as the Wall Street Journal or similar. Include a number of articles.

8. As you read and consider, capture the major themes and accomplishments your stories describe.

9. Present to large group.

10. As a large group, consider and organize what you have learned from the previous steps by creating a paragraph which clarifies where you and your organization intend to be in the coming years.

Vision - Criteria:

Envisioned Future: BHAGS; Big Hairy Audacious Goals

- "This rare ability to manage continuity and change - requiring a conscientiously practiced discipline - is closely linked to the ability to develop a vision. Vision provides guidance about what core to preserve and what future to simulate progress toward.

- "What we aspire to become, to achieve, to create - something that will require significant change and progress to attain."

- Consists of two parts: a 10-30 year audacious goal plus vivid descriptions of what it will be like to achieve the goal. (CP p.73).

- "There is a big difference between having a goal and becoming committed to a huge, daunting challenge..." (CP p.73).

- "Clear, compelling, serves as a unifying focal point of effort; acts a catalyst for team spirit." (CP p.73).

- "People get it right away; it takes little or no explanation." (CP p.73).

- Vivid description and a few key points (CP p.74).

- Passion, emotion, conviction (CP p.74).

- Does it get our juices flowing; doe we find it stimulating; Does it spur forward momentum; Does it get people going? (CP p.75).

- "Some executives make more progress by starting with the vivid description and backing from there into the BHAG" (CP p.75).

- "to create an effective envisioned future a certain level of unreasonable confidence and commitment" (CP p.75).

- "Should create a bit of the 'gulp' factor" (CP p.75)

(C/P), James C. Collins, and Jerry I. Porras, (1996); "Building Your Company's Vision;" Harvard Business Review September-October 1996, pp. 65-77.

Vision - Examples: (CP)

- Wal-Mart, 1990: become a $125 billion company by the year 2000

- Ford Motor, early 1900's: democratize the automobile

- Sony early, 1950's: become the company most know for changing the worldwide poor-quality image of Japanese products.

- Citibank, predecessor to Citicorp, 1915: Become the most powerful, the most far-reaching world financial institution that has ever been.

- Boeing, 1950: Become the dominant player in commercial aircraft, bring the world into the jet age.

- Philip Morris, 1950's: Knock off RJR as the number one tobacco company in the world..

- Watkins-Johnson, 1996: Become as respected in 20 years as Hewlett-Packard is today.

- Stanford University, 1940's: Become the Harvard of the West.

- General Electric Company, 1980's: Become number one or number two in every market we serve and revolutionize this company to have strengths of a big company combined with the leanness and agility of a small company.

- Rockwell, 1995: Transform this company from a defense contractor into the best diversified high-technology company in the world.

- Components Support Division of a computer products company, 1989: Transform this division from a poorly respected internal products supplier to one of the most respected, exciting, and sought after divisions in the company.

Vision - Considerations:

Visions that incorporate BHAGS provide stretch goals. Why does this help? If a leadership team provides an incremental goal to their organization, the organization can tweak some of the contributing factors and achieve the goal without much effort.

To state a stretch goal, to which to employees "gulp" signifying their surprise, requires an organization to innovate, not just improve. The stretch goal cannot be achieved with even an improved current process or capability. A new source of support must be created to achieve the goal requiring innovation. So while the employees may be uncomfortable for a while, this is one cost of change.

Vision – Format Option:

I prefer that the planning team present the metric portion of their Vision as a target list of 5-Year Objectives

Strategic Plan			Vision
Objectives	Year 1	Years 2-4	Year 5
Improve market share			45%
Improve profitability			21%
Improve employee retention			95%
Improve community reputation			#1 via sur-veys

Exercise 5: Business Environment Analysis (Comprehensive)

Business Environment: "playing field; even and uneven;" listing of internal and external promoting and restraining forces.

This exercise is the most complicated and time consuming exercise in my process. Some clients choose to complete it, some not. The questions and forms are intended to provide a comprehensive format to help the whole planning team establish a shared understanding of where their organization fits in the market. As you read through the instructions appreciate that no one person can or should provide all the data. Like other ideation forms, it serves as a brainstorming format to collect and arrange data to help teams make decisions. The final chart is a great junk drawer for the following steps: objectives, strategies, and actions.

Components and Interrelationships - Steps to consider:

- 5a. Market considerations – product/customer matrix.
- 5b. Market considerations – voice of the customer, trends.
- 5c. Market considerations Competitors – Their support to your product/customer matrix.
- 5d. Market considerations – differentiation factors.
- 5e. Capacity considerations – core process review.
- 5f. Capacity considerations – boundaries: corporate, regulatory, political, technology, etc.
- 5g Promoting and restraining forces.

Exercise 5 - Business Environment Considerations Matrix – Example

Our goal in this step is to build shared understanding of what is really going on in your market.

You are encouraged to pursue any resources that will complement your work.

- **Shared understanding:** an improved understanding of the breadth and depth of an issue as a result of dialogue.

- **Point of view:** a person's particular way of looking at things, their paradigm. Our paradigms are the result of the interaction of our conditioned perceptual skills and reinforced experiences.

- **Conflict:** discovery of different points of view.

- **Challenge:** an impersonal request to consider an alternative point of view.

- **Fallibility:** accepting your fallibility celebrates you're not quite done with who you can be.

- **Dialogue vs. discussion:** team members actively listen to understand others' points of view, and speak to describe their point of view while working to build a common understanding. Dialogue can describe the kind of conversation which builds a synergistic new and better understanding of an issue. Discussion describes the kind of conversation which only presents and compares current points of view.

This chart completed provides an excellent reference to subsequent planning process steps: goals/objectives, strategies, and actions.

5a. Market considerations – product/customer matrix:

TO DO:

- **Column title cells:** enter customer's names.
- **Row title cells:** enter your products that support the listed customers.

5b. Market considerations – voice of the customer, trends:

Customers' Wants / Products	ABC	DEF	GHI	
	• Low cost • Quality • Pgm Mgmt	• Cost	• Cost • Pgm Mgmt • Quality	• Service • Quality • Cost
A				
B	F RE / ABC + Losing mkt share + Late eng. changes + Financial distress + Pay bills	F RE / DEF + Big - Pay to play	F RE / GHI + More changes + Easy to work with + Demanding of Tier 1s + Eng / Purch coordin. - Small guy on block	F RE / JKL + Mkt share + Work w/you (a SPM) + DPV winning in mkt race + Win + Not last minute
C				

TO DO:

- **Column title cells:** enter customer's preferences beneath their names.
- **Intersecting cells:** enter what you do well/do poorly to support the listed customers in each applicable row.

5c. Market considerations Competitors – Their support to your product/customer matrix (next page):

	OUR COMPANY	OUR COMPANY	OUR COMPANY		
	• #1 supplier				Cautions abc
Δ	• Quality commitment	Δ • Launch execution • Cost reduction	• New guy		
	ABC • Risbourding + • (Lost leader)	DEF + • Cost reduction • Eng credibility • Good mkt	GHI + • Full system • See ← • Know DCX	OPS	MNO Cautic
Competition	Δ • Lots of debt	Δ • ?	Δ		• Gettin • Cost I
	LPS + • Nothing • Good mkt	DSP + • Fast • New, small • Tech expert • Play against KSP	DSP + • D connection • Aggressive pricing	QXP	LSP
Δ	• Commercially weak • No XDF product	Δ • Risk of new player	Δ • Unproven in NA		Castig • New t • Aggre
	DSP + • Nothing (Labor agmt)	WPS + • capability pardon (Labor contract)	ABC + • Not much: as APW	SYN	ABC • Big en • If fixed
Δ	• High cost • Poor Q. cost	Δ • Cost	Δ • As WAP		
	WPS + • mfg eng reputation	XLT + • Price			
Δ	• Not full system	Δ • Service			
Customers' Wants Products	ABC • Low cost • Quality • Pgm Mgmt	DEF • Cost	GHI • Cost • Pgm Mgmt • Quality	JKL • Service • Quality • Cost	

TO DO:

- Working in columns, list competitors who also support your listed customers. Include what each competitor does well/does poorly in supporting each client.

5d. Market considerations – differentiation factors:

Exercise 5 - Business Environment Considerations Matrix – E:

	OUR COMPANY	OUR COMPANY	OUR COMPANY		
+	• Commercial strength • #1 supplier	• System expertise +	• Tech competence + • Price		
Δ	• Quality • Delivery of commitment	Δ • Launch execution • Cost reduction	Δ • New guy		Caut
+	ABC • Rebourding • (Lost leader)	DEF + • Eng credibility • Good mkt	GHI • See ← • Know DCX	OPS	XL
Competition	Δ • Lots of debt	Δ • ?	Δ		
	LPS	DSP	DSP	QXP	

TO DO:

- Working in columns, while considering information listed below, how can you differentiate your product/service from the listed competitors. Include those characteristics that you want to maintain, and those you need to improve.

5e. Capacity considerations – core process review:

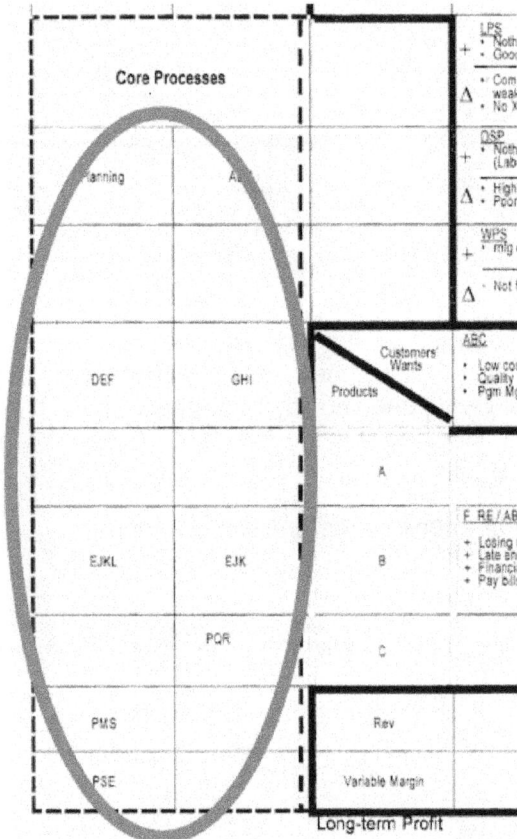

TO DO:

- To assist you in considering what you will do to improve your support to your customers, list the processes which support the products listed to the right.

5f. Capacity considerations – boundaries: corporate, regulatory, political, technology, etc.:

Cautions about Competitors

MNO	PQR
utions	• May wake u
• Getting aggressive Cost leader	
SP	WPS
Cautions	• Who are their partners, purchase
• New tech ctr • Aggressive	
ABC	ZTM
• Big enough to regard • If fixing costs	• If w/WQP (Need help)
	PXR
	• Have SCP

TO DO:

- Brainstorm and enter any issues that may affect your success moving forward. This can include governmental constraints, union issues, political issues, social issues, etc. These entries are not coordinated with the position of other entries on the chart.

5g. Financial Results:

		F_RE / ABC	F_RE / DEF	F_RE / GHI	F_RE / JKL
	A				
EJK	B	+ Losing mkt share + Late eng. changes + Financial distress + Pay bills	+ Big - Pay to play	+ More changes + Easy to work with + Demanding of Tier 1s + Eng / Purch coordin - Small guy on block	+ Mkt share + Work w/you (a SPM) + DPV w/rhing in + mkt race - Win + Not last minute
OR	C				
		Rev	$120M	$87M	$5M	$0
		Variable Margin	42%	44%	50%	0%
		Long-term	44%	38%	40%	

TO DO:

- List the financial results that warrant your attention.

Exercise 5h. Business Environment Analysis:

This exercise is similar to a SWOT analysis (Strengths/ Weaknesses/Opportunities/Threats) Its purpose is to identify components and affecting forces of what makes the business tick.

Exercise Process:

As a team facing a flip chart, at the top of the flip chart:

1. Document <u>audience</u> of this document.
2. Document <u>purpose</u> of this document.

3. Document <u>criteria</u> of this document.

You will develop data for four quadrants:

- Internal promoting.
- Internal restraining.
- External promoting.
- External restraining.

Complete the following instructions for each quadrant, one at a time.

Alone:

4. Writing one idea per Post-It note, silently brainstorm your ideas.

Factors to Consider – Examples:

- market size
- growth
- volatility
- customers
- competitors
- suppliers
- owners
- communities
- partners
- STEEP: social, technical, environmental, economic, political
- critical uncertainties

- trends, trend breaks
- long range, issues with long tails
- demography (aging, immigration)
- values (lifestyles)
- technological innovations and breakthroughs
- economic growth
- industry competitive structures
- legislation and regulation
- emergent rules (standards, trade practices)
- forces behind listed factors

As a team facing a flip chart

5. Place your entries on the flip chart one idea at a time, one person at a time.

6. Discuss and rank the items by impact on your business.

Example

Internal Promoting	Internal Restraining
1. strong staff	1. billable hours
2. firm commitment	2. diverse agendas
3. helpful partners	
4. talent pool	

External Promoting	External Restraining
1. limited competition	1. employment rate
2. market interest	2. e business buzz
3. referring clients	3. dispersion of client location
4. client loyalty	

Note: As you write your upcoming Objectives, Strategies and Actions, use this chart as a reference.

Each initiative (Objectives, Strategies, Actions) must

be able to survive in the business environment listed above, taking full advantage of the promoting forces, and minimizing the effects of the restraining forces.

Additional task (Objectives, Strategies, Actions) filters include Mission and Principles.

Exercise 6. Objectives

Document Format Consideration:

Somewhere within the following three levels of initiatives you will want to clarify **WHO** will do **WHAT** by **WHEN** with **SUCCESS AS MEASURED BY** needing **WHAT RESOURCES**

One way to do this: Use **SMARTR** criteria to write useful Objectives Strategies. And/or Actions:

S: Specific: Are we clear about what is to be done? Clearly states the expected outcome or result for which an employee will be held accountable. The outcome is linked to overall business objectives.

M: Measurable: How will we know if it has been achieved? States the criteria that will be used to measure performance and make sure that the objective has been accomplished.

A: Accountable: Do we have the capabilities to be successful? Falls within an employee's primary area of responsibilities. Or Aligned, is this initiative aligned with the organization's other goals.

R: Realistic; Reasonable chance of achievement.

T: Time bound; When does it have to be completed? States the specific time frame in which it is to be accomplished.

R: Resources needed.

Examples:

Objective Level

- FROM: Improve business.
- TO: TK will generate 15% increase in billings in xyz market segment by January 2002. Budget $1.5M, two project leaders.

Strategy Level

- FROM: Stay current in xyz field.
- TO: SJ will attend four legal seminars in the next 12 months (at least one of which is business or technology oriented. Budget $2000 per event.

Exercise 6: Objectives

"What to do next;" specific milestones of what must be accomplished in the next year to support the Vision; macro set of Objectives with measurables.

Exercise Process:

As a team facing a flip chart, at the top of the flip chart

1. Document <u>audience</u> of this document.

2. Document <u>purpose</u> of this document.

3. Document <u>criteria</u> of this document.

Alone:

4. Writing one idea per Post-It note, silently brainstorm ideas. Considering the promoting and restraining forces from Exercise 5, and all the previous documents, what needs to be done in the coming year?

As a team facing a flip chart

5. Place your entries on the flip chart one idea at a time, one person at a time.

6. Discuss and organize the entries into groups.

7. Identify the titles to the groups.

8. The group titles represent the objectives. Format the group titles to include action verbs.

Examples:

Objective # 1. Eradicate polio

Objective # 2. Advance the internal and external recognition and public image of RI

Format Option:

I encourage planning teams to present their Objectives as a target list of 1-Year Objectives considered alongside 2-4 Objectives and 5-Year Objectives (Vision).

Strategic Plan			Vision
Objectives	Year 1	Years 2 - 4	Year 5
Improve market share	20%	35%	45%
Improve profitability	11%	16%	21%
Improve employee retention	80%	87%	95%
Improve community reputation	#3 via surveys	#2 via surveys	#1 via surveys

Exercise 7: Strategies

"How to" accomplish Objectives while considering business environment requirements.

Exercise Process:

In a client situation I copy the previous exercises' Objective Post Its, usually 3-5, and place them individually at the top of separate flip charts. Then I assign participants in groups of two or three to complete the Strategies (usually 3-5 for each Objective) for their Objective.

Once the flip chart is set up with the Objective at the top, I still like to give the participants time to develop their own ideas about how to complete the Objective.

1. Writing one idea per Post-It note, silently brainstorm ideas that describe initiatives that would support completing the Objective.

As a team facing a flip chart

2. Place your entries on the flip chart one idea at a time, one person at a time.

3. Discuss and organize the entries into groups.

4. Identify the titles to the groups.

5. The titles of the groups are your Strategies. Format to include action verbs.

Once all the Objective/Strategy flip charts are completed, each team presents their results to the whole planning team for discussion, revision, and buy off.

Example below: two tiers of details (Objectives and Strategies): Rotary International.

Objective # 1. Eradicate polio.

Strategies:

1. Support the plans and goals of the International Polio Plus Committee.

2. Maintain and promote Rotarian participation in Polio Plus Partners.

3. Continue to focus our collaborative relationships on the ultimate goal of polio eradication.

Objective # 2. Advance the internal and external recognition and public image of RI

Strategies:

1. Conduct internal and external public information campaigns to deepen global awareness of Rotary International and its programs.

2. Engage leadership at all levels in telling the world about Rotary commitments and outcomes.

Exercise 8: Action Plans

"To do assignments;" quarterly, prioritized action steps necessary to support the Objectives and Strategies.

In the vast majority of my client situations, the Actions are developed by those employees who report to the planning session participants. In this case the Objectives/ Strategies are assigned to appropriate planning team members who complete the Action exercises for each of the Objectives' Strategies they've been assigned. The actions should include sufficient format so readers and initiative owners know WHO will do WHAT by WHEN with SUCCESS AS MEASURED BY.

(AB, CD, etc. = individuals, project owners)

1. Objective: Build a network which generates 60% billings by January, 20XX.

> 1a. Strategy: Identify and establish a contact program for two referral sources.
>> 1a1. Action Plan: AB Attend Joint seminars; one per quarter;$3000.
>> 1a2. Action Plan: CD complete Mailing list contacts; update monthly: $200.
>
> 1a3. Action Plan: MJ attend referral source sponsored programs; one per quarter; $2500.
>
> 1b. Identify 5-10 clients or potential clients for the contact program.
> 1b1. LK establish and calendar a plan for quarterly contact.(Lunches, breakfasts, entertainment) $0.
>> 1b2. GI conduct 3 off-the-clock visits to client location; $150.

Note: As you write your Objectives, Strategies and Actions, use the Business Environment chart (exercise 5 summary) as a reference.

Each initiative must be able to survive in the business environment listed, taking full advantage of the promoting forces, and minimizing the effects of the restraining forces.

Additional task filters include Mission and Principles and other planning documents.

Exercise 9 - Plan Implementation Considerations

The challenge here is to turn decisions into plans into calendar entries into action and project success. This exercise helps the planning team to consider how they will successfully use the new plan to positively guide the organization in the coming months.

One way to proliferate a strategic plan is to let other groups in the organization review and influence the plan before it is finalized. One approach is called the "W" process.

Exercising the "W" process in strategic planning includes many levels of leaders to develop and implement a strategic plan.

"W" Process

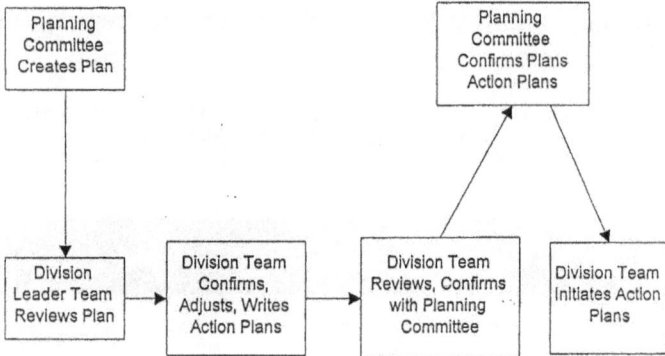

Exercise nine also includes assignments for the finance support teams to work and broadcast the budgets necessary to support the new plan.

Exercise 10 - Plan Monitoring Considerations:

Here the planning team selects the process and schedule of leadership meeting agenda items that will impose the task of reviewing the plan's progress.

Additional Supporting Tools – Presentation Scoring

In some larger organizations, different groups within the organization provide updates about their respective teams. The following process is helpful when planning team members are presenting to each other. The goal is to build great plans which are by themselves substantive and feasible, and that the plans together are aligned and synergistic.

Each planning team member should consider the following four criteria when listening to and evaluating this session's strategic plans.

Our focus is on the substance of the plan, not the delivery.

A) *Would you commit your limited and valuable resources to this plan?*

4 - without a doubt
3 – with a few reservations (list on your scoring sheet)
2 – with a number of reservations (list on your scoring sheet)
1 – no (list your reasons on your scoring sheet)

B) *Is the plan complete and of high quality; how many open issues and questions?*

4 - without a doubt
3 – with a few reservations (list on your scoring sheet)
2 – with a number of reservations (list on your scoring sheet)
1 – no (list your reasons on your scoring sheet)

C) *Does the plan complement the overall objectives and strategies for your organization?*

4 - without a doubt
3 – with a few reservations (list on your scoring sheet)
2 – with a number of reservations (list on your scoring sheet)
1 – no (list your reasons on your scoring sheet)

D) What is the plan's chance of success?

4 or 5 = High
2 or 3 = Medium
0 or 1 = low

A plan may require a high commitment of resources, be well thought out, meet the objectives but still carry a high risk of success, thereby giving it a high mark if the risk is mitigated by the potential gains. A plan's final score is the sum of the four scores.

If this were a plan to build a racing boat: "Do I think that this boat will float and be able to compete, and here's how I'd improve it." Questions about the plans as a collection can include "Do these plans fit together, are they collectively robust and synergistic, will they work together in our system and culture?" Our dialogue around the plans has the purpose of building plans worthy of earning "3s" "4s."

5
Introduce Scenario Planning Skills

I learned how to facilitate scenario planning with Peter Schwartz, author of *Art of the Long View* through the Global Business Network (*www.gbn.com*).

Chapters five and six will help you build skills to be more creative in a business sense (vs. artistic). Strategic planning most often support generating ideas that concern current issues. Scenario planning skills support generating ideas that concern not only the future, but multiple alternative futures.

	Tactical	*Strategic*
Improve *(Convergent)*	Process Improvement Skills	Strategic Planning
	Collaboration Skills	
Innovate *(Divergent)*	Creative Thinking Skills	Scenario Planning

Ideation Skills – Creativity – Review

Please review Chapter 2 – Fundamental Strategy, especially about precipitating events.

Strategic Planning vs. Scenario Planning

Strategic Planning: Create an operational planning document that guides company leaders and employees, and improve the executive team's ability to identify, prioritize, and assign opportunities, and contribute to improved company performance. Leadership team members select high impact alternatives while building support necessary for successful implementation.

Scenario Planning: This "thinking around the corner" meeting helps teams to consider alternative futures, not trying to predict the future, but prepare for a successful response plan no matter what happens, The value of this technique comes from the deep dialogue that the different scenario stories provoke. The alternate views generate new insights about a company and its possible futures. Thinking this way helps prepare the contributors to notice and consider emerging ideas before others even perceive any change.

Scenario Planning is an excellent complement and second step to effective Strategic Planning.

One goal of these two planning strategies is to create an operational planning document that guides company leaders and employees, and improve the executive team's ability to identify, prioritize, and assign opportunities, and contribute to improved company performance. Another goal of these two planning strategies is to continue to discuss, evaluate, and reprioritize which factors warrant the leadership team's attention, which factors managed generate the best results for the organization. While a strategic plan can represent a current set of goals to reach a larger set of goals, scenario planning can build the understanding of and support for changes to the plan to further improve a strategic plan's results.

Scenario Planning Introduction

One view of what differentiates successful organizations from less successful organizations is the quality and quantity of the decisions the successful organization makes and implements.

Improved Company Performance
↑
Improved Decisions, Behaviors
↑
Improved Insights and Ideas
↑
Improved Thinking

Decision making is a process. A crucial process. It determines how organizations choose to do one thing vs. another, with successful and not-so-successful results associated with each. One thing we have learned since 1980 is that the result in any situation is the consequence of the contributing processes. Strong results are the consequence of strong processes. The converse is also true. As cited in other *Good Thinking Series* books:

"Brilliant process management is our strategy. We get brilliant results from average people managing brilliant processes. We observe that our competitors often get average (or worse) results from brilliant people managing broken processes."
—Mr. Cho, Vice Chairman of Toyota

Scenario planning is a structured method which promotes better decision making and support by provoking a team to think about the future in a variety of ways, good, bad, and in between.

The significant benefit of this technique comes from the deep dialogue that the different scenario stories provoke. The alternate views generate new insights about a company and its future. Having thought of this arrangement of business factors and resulting actions, if or when some portions of any of the futures actually comes into play, which they often do, the team is ready to notice the change, respond, and act - and far sooner than their competitors who had not done this hard thinking.

Many company leaders wish they had a crystal ball to look into to help them see and consider the future. "If we had just known that this was going to happen, we could have been ready." And while this capability does not seem to be currently available, there is a structured meeting technique that comes pretty close: scenario planning.

Scenario planning is an effective dialogue technique that helps develop strategic direction for an organization. Scenario planning is a strategic conversation methodology which does not replace your current planning process, but rather complements it.

Many current strategic planning processes ask you to imagine what the future will be like and then write a plan to help you achieve your goals. As a sailor doesn't tie-off the rudder of their boat after pushing away from the pier, you've noticed that things change, just about as soon as you complete your plan.

The purpose of scenario planning is to help you imagine and consider a number of possible, plausible futures. This includes helping you to think around the corner, to get past the obvious, and find the important factors that will affect your business and decision making which are currently off your radar screen.

Scenario planning helps you to think these possible futures through separately, consider their implications, and even identify leading indicators which you can research from news stories, business reports, and the like, to allow you to know if part of one of the futures is beginning to come into play.

And yes, while you do have to decide and write a plan, scenarios help you prepare for the inevitable evolving combination of imagined futures. Having considered a variety of alternatives before you committed, you are then ready to be open to new information, flexible in your confidence you've thought through what to do in each case, and ready to respond quickly with improvements to your plan, rather than late to react. You've prepare yourself for whatever might happen.

The process asks a team to consider a future, as many of its components as they can think of, how they might play out in a particular business environment, and most importantly, what they would do if that future came into play.

Peter Schwartz, author of *The Art of the Long View - Paths to Strategic Insight for Yourself and Your Company,* describes scenarios as "stories which describe different, though equally plausible, futures. Together, they are a tool for ordering one's perceptions about alternative future environments in which one's decisions might be played out."

The executive summary of scenario planning might read: efficient and effective dialogue technique which helps participants generate valuable insights about how a company works within itself, with its customers, suppliers, partners, etc, and how it might deal with a number of possible futures. These insights come from the unusual connections made in responding to the questions that support scenario planning.

One important distinction, the difference between discussion and dialogue. In dialogue, meeting participants actively listen to understand others' points of view, and speak to describe their point of view while working to build a shared understanding. Dialogue can describe the kind of conversation which builds a synergistic new and better understanding of an issue. Discussion describes the kind of conversation which only presents and compares current points of view and all too often deteriorates into turf and ego battles providing poor decisions about the future, and weak support for any of the decisions.

One way to consider the value of scenario planning asks us to imagine there are three kinds of decisions and behaviors:

- Intelligent
- Emotional
- Instinctive

When people are stressed they most often default to emotion or instinctive behaviors and often making decisions they later regret.

Using effective thinking processes like scenario planning help keep people thinking more intelligently.

Scenario Planning - Additional Considerations

The most productive users are individuals and teams that value a structured process which promotes deep thinking and the many insights it generates. A team can conduct scenario planning anytime they are considering their options around a particularly important issue. In conjunction with strategic planning, I most often conduct scenario planning after strategic planning, asking, "Should we follow this strategic plan?"

Considering the notion, "You cannot realize what you cannot imagine," scenario planning is a dialogue tool that, facilitated well, generates insights, promoting and provoking, that while your head may spin, you will be very glad you "thought of that."

What you notice is that after you have discussed something, paid attention to it, and even though it may have seemed trivial at the time, you often will recall the idea and associated conversation when the topic comes up again. The fancy term for this is cognitive association (I think).

In my world it's called, "The White Jetta Phenomenon." Many years ago, we bought our oldest daughter a very used white Jetta. I never paid any particular attention to these cars before we bought one. After that, whoa, they're everywhere. Driving down the street, "Hey, there's Robin," wave, wave, oops, not her. I mean, I couldn't believe how many white Jettas there were in West Michigan after I bought one.

The enormous advantage a scenario planning participant/contributor has is that they store many, many ideas, possible actions, and suspected results during a session. Then as the future unfolds, portions of these considered futures begin to come into play. You, having thought of it during a scenario planning session, notice it, and can then respond to the issue should it warrant your attention. If you have not thought about it before, well, all those white Jettas will just pass you by. Not having had the dialogue from a thinking session like this, great leaders may not notice something that is beginning to happen, coming at you all day long in news stories, newspaper articles, conversations, etc.

Scenario Planning – Preparation Considerations

As with any meeting, it is best that the participants are prepared. Tactical meetings usually provide an agenda of predictable questions. This is fundamentally convergent. With four options in front of the team, choose the best one. Strategic planning meetings usually provide an agenda of predictable questions (Mission, Principles, Scoreboard, etc). This is also more convergent than divergent; planning teams often have ten things they'd really like to do over the coming year, but the time and resource to do 5 or 6.

Scenario planning meetings, like creative thinking skills sessions, are deliberately divergent. You start with a few options you are familiar with and use a structured process that imposes some great precipitating events (see chapter two). To be prepared to be able to respond to the precipitating events (great provoking questions) each participant will do well to broaden and deepen their understanding of contributing variables, and flexibility to consider these variable together in new, unusual, and productive ways.

The best results come when all team members have really done their homework before they meet for the scenario planning session. Your team's new business ideas resulting from the scenario planning session will likely be an unexpected combination of ideas of the participants. It's important that you come with your own data-based ideas. In earlier comments about creativity, I called this the junk drawer. It may just look like a lot of stuff, but viewed in the context of a problem, solutions (new combinations of items) seem to jump out at you. But you've got to have a great junk drawer to consider.

Preparation options for scenario planning are the same as those listed in Chapter 3 for strategic planning.

Scenario Planning - Preparation Exercises

For a full session, 3-4 days, the following questions can be asked in one-on-one interviews a week or two before the session. (from my 1998 *Global Business Network* scenario planning seminar notes):

1. *Clairvoyant:* if I could answer any questions for you, what would you want to know?

2. *Good Scenario:* if you looked back from 10 years hence and told the triumph of this organization, what would be the story? Why?

3. *Bad Scenario:* If you look back from 10 years hence and told the failure of this organization, what would be the story, Why?

4. *Lessons From the Past:* What does this company "need to forget?" What must it remember?

5. *Important Decisions Ahead:* What are one or two critical strategic decisions on the immediate horizon?

6. *Constraints in the System:* What are the obstacles here? To this process? To the "triumph" story?

7. *Epitaph:* How would you like this company to be remembered? Your own role?

8. *Success:* How do you define a "successful strategy?" What elements/criteria do you look for?

9. **Closure:** What should I have asked you that I didn't?

Scenario Planning Session Materials

- Exercise Guide includes details on each process step. Chapter six of this book.
- Post Its
- Markers
- Flip charts
- Flip chart tape
- Data you brought
- Any resources you can find and use

Scenario Planning Process Overview: Steps 1-10 (Brief Summary)

Detailed instructions follow in chapter six.

1. Document your organization's scoreboard issue.
2. Identify Issue, decision to be made:
   - Decisions that affect business.
   - Keep you awake at night.
3. List Key Factors - mini, micro:
   - That affect the above decisions.
   - What do you want to know in make these decisions?
4. List Driving Forces - macro:
   - Social
   - Technical

- Economic
- Environment
- Politics
- Predetermined elements
- Critical uncertainties
- That influence key factors
- Trends, trend breaks
- Forces behind #3
- Research required

5. Rank by Importance and Uncertainty:

- Consider both lists #3 and #4 together.
- Note: you do not discard the remaining ideas; they can be incorporated into any appropriate scenario you develop.

6. Select Scenario Logic:

- Into themes, plots of stories.

10 Years Out	5 Years Out	1 Year Out	1 Year Out	5 Years Out	10 Years Out
		High Price	*Fuel*		
Neo Traditional Values					*Inner-Directed Values*
		Low Price	*Fuel*		
10 Years Out	5 Years Out	1 Year Out	1 Year Out	5 Years Out	10 Years Out

7. Flesh Out Scenario:

   • Generate narratives.

   • How could end points happen?

8. Identify Implications of Scenarios on Decisions

   • Decisions per scenarios.

   • Compare decisions to scenarios.

   • Does it fit, risk, robust?

   • Decisions that affect business.

   • Keep you awake at night.

9. Select Leading Indicators, Sign Posts:

   • Link indicator movement to implications.

10. Answer question listed in #1 above.

Steps 1-8 Summary - Wall Set Up

The following two diagrams represent the six (or more) flip charts that should be posted in the planning room across the wall at the beginning of the scenario planning session. This provides the shared work space for the planning session.

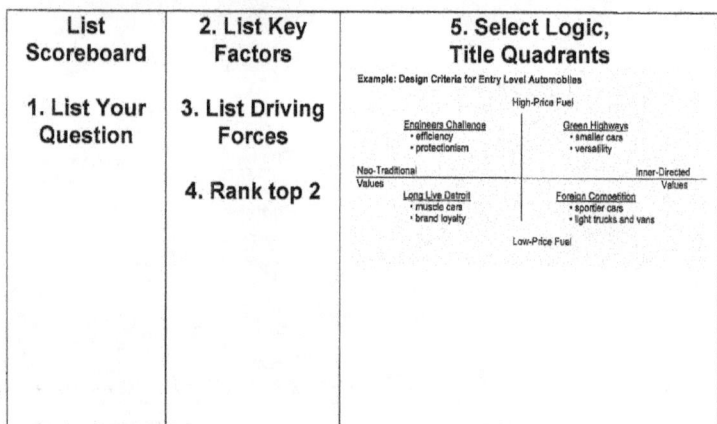

List Scoreboard	2. List Key Factors	5. Select Logic, Title Quadrants
1. List Your Question	**3. List Driving Forces**	Example: Design Criteria for Entry Level Automobiles

	4. Rank top 2	High-Price Fuel
		
		Engineers Challenge Green Highways
		• efficiency • smaller cars
		• protectionism • versatility
		
		Neo-Traditional Inner-Directed
		Values Values
		   Long Live Detroit Foreign Competition
		     • muscle cars • sportier cars
		     • brand loyalty • light trucks and vans
		
		Low-Price Fuel

6. Fill In Scenarios	7. Indentify Implications	8. Select Leading Indicators

10 Years Out	5 Years Out	1 Year Out	1 Year Out	5 Years Out	10 Years Out
		High Price	*Fuel*		
Neo Traditional Values					*Inner-Directed Values*
		Low Price	*Fuel*		
10 Years Out	5 Years Out	1 Year Out	1 Year Out	5 Years Out	10 Years Out

6
Practice Scenario Planning Skills

Step 1. Document your target organization's scoreboard

PROCESS:

I like to start the session by documenting the organization's "success as measured by." Some companies call them KPIs. With the scoreboard documented, it serves as a reference point as the planning team develops the four or more scenario stories; "If this future were to happen, what would the scoreboard look like then?"

Working as a team, document on a flip chart your organization's goals and indicators with a Scoreboard presented on a flip chart. Use the brainstorming process with Post Its described earlier.

Example Criteria

- **Scoreboard:** QCDISM (success as measured by...).
- **Quality:** defects, complaints, rework, etc.
- **Cost:** operations costs, warranty, etc.

- **Delivery:** on-time, right product/right place/right time, etc.

- **Innovation:** new products, improvements, new business, etc.

- **Safety:** days without accident, hours lost time, etc.

- **Morale**: absenteeism, tardiness, turnover, etc.

Example:

- **Quality:** complaints on fewer than 5% orders, measurable improvement on 75% of our processes.

- **Cost:** operating at or below operating expense plans.

- **Current Programs:** supporting 15 programs as outlined in 2001 strategic plan.

- **New Programs:** supporting 2 new programs per half year as outlined in 2001 strategic plan.

- **Employee Morale:** employee turnover less than 10% per year.

Extra Credit

A "Balanced Scorecard" includes both leading and lagging measurables.

- Leading indicators can include learning and growth, internal business processes, and proactive customer support.

- Financial performance is a lagging indicator.

Step 2. Document Question

Identify an issue and format it as the decision to be made.

This approach to scenario planning is based on choosing steps that provide focus to the dialogue. While some planning leaders might gather around a table and ask each other to imagine some different scenarios, and then talk about them, this approach asks the planning team to as early as possible begin to target the topic of their scenario planning conversation.

These decisions are ones that affect business, decisions that keep you awake at night, the ones that answered will have a very high impact on your business. Keep the decision to five to fifteen words and to a five to ten year view. Less than five years is not divergent enough.

Optional Types:

1. Decision focus: do/not do.
2. Strategy development focusing on firm, division, region.
3. Revise/rethink core business.
4. Exploratory: learning, team building.

Examples:

- Should we build a new $600M facility?
- Is the basic long-term strategy of the company oriented properly?
- Should we make a particular investment?
- Should we introduce a new consumer product that is highly sensitive to (criteria)?

Step 3. List Key Factors (mini, micro) that affect the above decision.

Here you are deciding what to talk about. Think about building a great junk drawer (collection of ideas that can be melded into potential new ideas) These factors describe what you want to know to make these decisions, everything that could make a difference. These factors are relatively obvious, close-at-hand factors in the micro-environment that influence the focal issue.

Process

Generate Ideas - Brainstorming

- Clarify the topic and process: Key Factors.

- Generate ideas. Use Post Its; one idea per sheet, large writing. Give each member five minutes alone to work quietly.

- Stand semi-circle at a flip chart.

- Discuss as you place your ideas on the flip chart. Each person presents one of their ideas at a time placing it on a flip chart titled Key Factors.

- Stack or tick-mark duplicate topic Post Its.

- Group if useful.

Considerations for ideas to include:

- Mix internal and external.

- Pull from SWOT (strengths, weaknesses, opportunities, threats) or +/- internal/external   forces.

- Include outsiders in steps 2, 3; push the boundaries.

- These are key factors are often on radar screen.

- Empty the barrel of the obvious.

Examples:

- Market size
- Growth
- Volatility
- Customers
- Competitors
- Suppliers
- Owners
- Communities
- Partners

Step 4 List Driving Forces (macro) that affect the above key factors.

Here you are digging deeper, wondering why the ideas listed in step three are on the list, and what actually are the driving forces behind the ideas. These forces, sometimes also called environmental forces, are relatively less obvious, more remote forces in the wider macro-environment. Key factors (step 3) are often on radar screen, environmental factors (step 4) often aren't. Look for those elements that affect the structural underpinnings of the future, the causes of the causes.

Process

Generate Ideas - Brainstorming

1. Clarify the topic and process: Key Factors.

2. Generate ideas. Use Post Its; one idea per sheet, large writing. Give each member 5 minutes alone to work quietly.

3. Stand semi-circle at a flip chart.

4. Discuss as you place your ideas on the flip chart. Each person presents one of their ideas at a time placing it on a flip chart titled Key Factors.

5. Stack duplicate topic Post Its.

Considerations:

- Causes of the causes.
- Searching for the unknown unknowns.
- Driving forces move the plot of the scenarios; come from outside to affect your business; obvious to one, invisible.
- Long range, issues with long tails.
- If we're not startled, gulping, etc., we're not onto the right issues.
- Try random pairing of forces to find new connections.

Examples:

- Forces behind Step 3's key factors.
- STEEP: social, technical, environmental, economic, political.
- Predetermined elements that influence key factors.
- Critical uncertainties.
- Trends, trend breaks.
- Long range, issues with long tails.
- Demography (aging, immigration).

- Values (lifestyles).

- Political or spiritual movements.

- Technological innovations and breakthroughs.

- Economic growth.

- Industry competitive structures.

- Legislation and regulation.

- Emergent rules (standards, trade practices).

- Michael Porter's:

    1. Power, vigor, competence of existing competitors.

    2. Power, vigor, competence of complementors.

    3. Power, vigor, competence of customers.

    4. Power, vigor, competence of suppliers.

    5. Possibility that what your business is doing can be done in a different way.

    6. Power, vigor, competence of potential competitors.

Step 5. Rank Key Factors AND Driving Forces by Importance and Uncertainty

You're now about to create the structure for the scenario stories. In this step you will choose the four box matrix's two axis titles (x-axis and y-axis).

We will try to find two factors from the combined list of ideas posted from steps 3 and 4 that are:

- High impact

- High uncertainty

These two factors should be significantly different from each other. Ideally the two factors pass the "gulp test:" if we're not startled, gulping, etc., we're not onto the right issues. We want two factors that will provoke our thinking, not just an opportunity to review same old information.

After a few sessions you will come to appreciate that it is also better to "place the stake precisely" vs. be concerned where precisely you place it. In other words, when it's time to choose the axis titles, it's more important that the four futures (quadrants) are clearly different from each other than we get the truly best two factors as axis titles.

You can and will use any of the ideas from exercise 3 and 4 to feed your stories in the four futures. And of course when you think of new ideas, include those also.

Step 6. Select Scenario Logic

You're now about to create the structure for the scenario stories. In this step you will develop four scenarios/stories based on your choice of the four box matrix's two axis titles (x-axis and y-axis) from step 5.

Scenario logics are plausible, separate, detailed, narrative stories based on characteristics of each scenario.

We will create a matrix to provide a scaffolding for your story telling with four quadrants.

The matrix coordinates (from step 5) are forces prioritized by critical uncertainties; choice criteria: relevant, novel, plausible. Choose more uncertain forces, extreme points.

The stories we will develop involve dialogue about relevant drivers. We will then develop our stories in quadrants, starting out 10 years, then five, then two year views as concentric arcs, like a target around the center of the matrix.

It is helpful to title each quadrant with a memorable name.

Here is an example. Fuel price and values were selected as the two axis titles. The adjectives for each describe how the factor is different along the range of the axis. This step can be completed on one flip chart.

Example: Design Criteria for Entry Level Automobiles

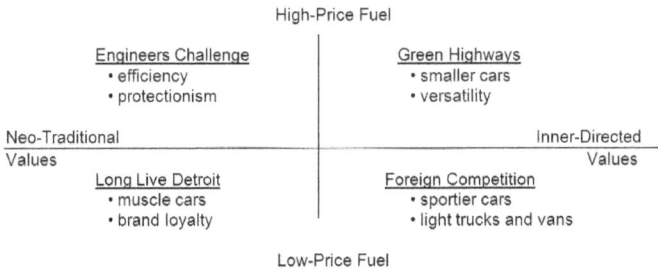

Example: Design Criteria for Entry Level Automobiles

High-Price Fuel

Engineers Challenge • efficiency • protectionism	Green Highways • smaller cars • versatility

Neo-Traditional   Inner-Directed
Values   Values

Long Live Detroit • muscle cars • brand loyalty	Foreign Competition • sportier cars • light trucks and vans

Low-Price Fuel

Scenario Quadrants; set up checks:

1. Are one or two quadrants completely implausible?

2. Can you see a high concept in each quadrant?

3. Are the stories in each quadrant interestingly different in ways that make a difference to the focal issue?

4. Can you find the official future quadrant or something close to it?

While considering all the items that you brainstormed earlier in steps 3 and 4, you will get back all the complexity you seem to have lost when whittling down over 50 factors to just two axes of uncertainty.

Step 7. Develop scenarios with remaining factors and forces

Set up an arrangement of four flip charts. One option has two on top, two on the bottom, long side along the top. Tape them together and then onto the wall. Duplicate the format titles listed below. Then develop a narrative for each quadrant covering 10, 5, and 1 year views (in that order, planning from the future), not just a description of an endpoint.

10 Years Out	5 Years Out	1 Year Out	1 Year Out	5 Years Out	10 Years Out
		High Price	*Fuel*		
Neo Traditional *Values*					*Inner-Directed* *Values*
		Low Price	*Fuel*		
10 Years Out	5 Years Out	1 Year Out	1 Year Out	5 Years Out	10 Years Out

Filling in the stories is a team effort, lots of open dialogue with a rotation of scribes. I ask that each team work first with the future most similar to the organization's current strategic plan, called the official future, working from the ten year out column, then the five year out column, and finally the one year our column. I ask that each column includes at least ten bulleted entries. It is helpful to describe the other three quadrants with specific names (high price fuel, inner-drected values, etc) so they can be discussed in comparisons.

I find it useful to set the exercise up by asking the team to take themselves mentally to a particular column and imagine that they are there, that this future has come to be. What sort of things would be reported in the media, what would people be talking about, etc?

Stick in one column at a time, do not jump around.

It can also be useful to use colored markers to separate types of data:

- black: data

And later we can use:

- red: challenges, threats
- blue: opportunities, strengths
- green: to do's

When finished we will ask, "Where are we today on this matrix? Where are we going to be?"

Step 8. Identify Implications of Scenarios on Decisions

With the wall chart of the four futures completed, it is now time to review your work and consider the implications of actions your organization would need to take as a result of the unfolding of each of the scenarios.

Now it's time to consider what we want to know about after this has happened, after the scenario has played out; what are the needs, needs which are extensions of earlier listed driving forces. If this scenario will come true, so what? Explore layers of meanings, and main categories, as well as focal issue, and further research.

Use colors/data type

- black: data
- red: challenges, threats
- blue: opportunities, strengths
- green: to do's

Process:

1. Take one scenario and believe it is the future.
2. Ask "what could we do, what should we do?"
3. Brainstorm your options-high level, strategic.
4. Agree on at least five.
5. Repeat of all other scenarios.

Consider Your Scoreboard from the first exercise

1. Make four small copies of your Scoreboard titles with Post Its or write them right on the flip chart, duplicates in each of the four quadrants.
2. Indicate with arrows how each scoreboard item would fare in this quadrant's future (up = better, sideways = neutral, down = worse).

Developing options-useful approach:

1. Return to present.
2. Review and discuss all options.
3. Anything robust across all scenarios (no brainers)?
4. List and number all remaining options.
5. Vote for those you think may have the most impact and greatest impact.

Considerations:

- From external environment, what is this world like?
- From industry, how does the industry evolve and adapt?
- From the firm, what does this mean for this firm?
- From business units, how does this impact specific business units or functions?
- Implications of what we want to know about after this has happened; in this scenario, what are the needs? Needs are extensions of earlier listed driving forces.
- In reading newspapers, having identified and discussed logic, newspapers will uncover that scenario logics is currently out there?
- This scenario will come true, so what? Explore layers of meanings, and main categories, as well as focal issue, and further research.

Step 9. Select Leading Indicators, Sign Posts

Identify indicators you can monitor to warn you a

scenario is beginning to play out.

These are often included in your results from Steps 2 and 3, Key Factors and Driving Forces.

Considerations:

- Little signs of big changes.
- Think upstream; looking for upstream reports.

Step 10. Answer question listed in #1 above

Developing Initiatives – Scenario Reviews

Materials:

1. Previous scenarios' text and diagrams.
2. Previous scenario's authors.
3. Any resources (data, thinkers, etc.) which shed light on events and forces that have come into play since the targeted scenarios were written.

Process:

1. Review scenario thinking and writing process.
2. Discuss and record what's changed since you wrote the original version. Consider any additions, corrections, deletions to the data in steps 1-7.
3. Lighten up.
4. As a large group, target your official future and work through step 7: Explore Implications and Options.

5. Pay particular attention to the detail of the components of your original question. For example, if you're looking to confirm/revise your strategic plan, compare the detail of your scenario dialogue with the detail of your plan. What might change, what might stay the same?

6. Regroup into smaller groups with the individual alternative scenarios' authors and work through Step 8: Explore Implications and Options, again paying attention to the detail of the components of your original question. If you complete your preparation early, read through the other two scenarios.

7. Meet as a large group presenting and considering your team's scenario. Work deliberately to confirm or revise your response to the details of your Step 1 question.

8. Consider and revise your Step 9: Early Indicators.

9. Your output is an answer to your original question, with possible detailed revisions if warranted.

Extra Credit:

1. Complete steps 1-8 around a component of your original Step 1 question.

2. Complete steps 1 - 8 starting with a clean slate.

7
Additional Ideation Tools and Techniques

Collaboration is a primary strategy to help improve company performance.

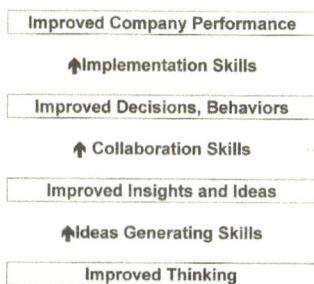

Improved Company Performance

↑Implementation Skills

Improved Decisions, Behaviors

↑ Collaboration Skills

Improved Insights and Ideas

↑Ideas Generating Skills

Improved Thinking

Productive collaboration requires dialogue to help build both an effective decision and cooperative support.

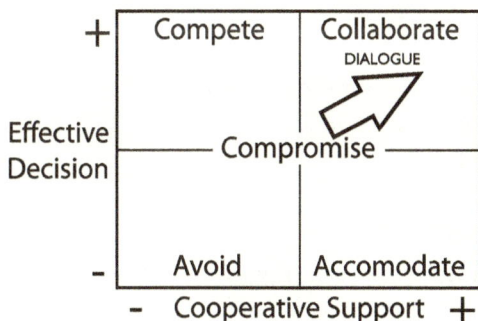

+	Compete	Collaborate
Effective Decision	Compromise	DIALOGUE
−	Avoid	Accomodate

− Cooperative Support +

Collaboration tools work because they:

a. Guide a person or team's thinking to develop dialogue to minimize the unhelpful behaviors (avoid, accommodate, compromise, and compete), engaging helpful behaviors (collaborate).

b. Focus on building a great decision using the best ideas, minimizing unnecessary personality friction.

c. Are very interactive and hands on to help build buy-in (people support what they help create).

"Collaboration is the process of shared creation—two or more individuals with complementary skills interacting to create a shared understanding that none had previously possessed or could have come to on their own."

—Michael Schrage, Research Fellow at the MIT, author of two critically-acclaimed books on collaboration

"If you want to teach people a new way of thinking, don't bother trying to teach them. Instead, give them a tool, the use of which will lead to new ways of thinking."

—Buckminster Fuller, American engineer, author, designer, inventor, and futurist

The following pages will provide introductions to a variety of tools I have found useful in helping teams collaborate during both strategic planning and scenario planning sessions.

In each case you can learn more from the many resources found on the internet by just listing the tool title in the search field.

1. AB See: page 128
2. Affinity Diagram: page 129
3. Andon cups: page 130

30. Six Thinking Hats (de Bono): page 174

31. Storyboard: page 175

32. Systematic Diagram: page 177

33. Thinking and Performance: page 178

34. Value Chain: page 180

35. Waste Search: page 181

There are many resources on the internet to help you learn more about these tools. For example Google web, images, and video.

AB See

"Did you hear what I think I said?"

AB See is a collaboration tool best used when two parties too often move to argument and rarely accomplish anything.

The goal is to establish dialogue. In dialogue each members actively listen to understand others' points of view, and speak to describe their point of view while working to build a shared understanding. Dialogue can describe the kind of conversation which builds a synergistic new and better understanding of an issue.

Ordinary discussion describes the kind of conversation which often only presents and compares current points of view. If positions and/or personalities are strong, it usually deteriorates to an argument.

AB See Exercise Instructions

1. Assemble two opposing persons in a room with a third person as a referee just in case things get testy.

2. Decide which opposing person is A and B.

3. Flip a coin to decide who goes first, let's say A.

4. A speaks while B can only listen while B take notes.

5. When A says they're done, B must report what they heard A said without any editing etc. When B is done, A must confirm B heard A. If not, B continues.

6. Reverse roles and repeat.

The beauty and effectiveness of this simple technique is that its structure when followed by the participants prevents an argument, maximizing the chance to be heard as well as hear.

In my experience, about 70% of the formerly arguing parties come to discover they had only a misunderstanding significantly improving their willingness and ability to work together in the future more productively.

AFFINITY DIAGRAM

OVERVIEW:

An Affinity Diagram is a sorting tool used to help identify "natural groupings" of data. It's easy to do this after you have completed brainstorming as I just outlined. A helpful observation after brainstorming: you likely do not have 30-40 different ideas, you probably have about six. The Affinity Diagram is merely an opportunity to recognize and consolidate these similar items. This helps you focus on fewer issues. The number of Post Its may indicate a level of importance.

PROCESS:

1. Have team members brainstorm an issue, writing each of their ideas on Post Its.

2. Place all of the collected brainstormed Post Its on a flip chart so all of them can be read at one time.

3. Team members begin to "sort" the Post Its, repositioning them so they are with other Post Its similar in idea, into their "natural groupings."

4. When all of the Post Its have been sorted into groupings, write header Post Its and place them at the top of the groupings.

5. Depending on the group, if there are likely one or two who would direct the process verbally if given a chance, I'll level the playing field and ask the team to complete this part of the exercise silently.

ANDON CUPS

A possible worldwide first: Meeting andon signals

Think of a meeting as a decision-making factory. You want your meetings to have no defects and no waste.

You may have heard of andon signals as an integral tool on a lean manufacturing floor, a simple light arrangement to provide feedback about a machine's current state—often in the customary traffic light arrangement: red, yellow, green.

These are operator driven, so if and when the employee finds a problem *they* change the light's status to alert the machine maintenance team to help immediately.

So why not use this in a meeting? I tried this first with a planning team who was working on a series of issues about which there was some strong opinions and disagreement.

I started the meeting as its facilitator, explaining the role of andon board on their manufacturing floor and then brought out my andon devices: simple colored plastic cups, stacked with green on top to start.

I explained how the colors worked to indicate their current level of support for the decision at hand, and encouraged them to keep themselves and me informed of their position on a real-time basis by changing the top cup as they saw fit.

We began the meeting, and clickety-click, the top cups changed colors and we were off. As the meeting progressed the cups changed to green, then to yellow, then back to green and so on. No red cups, to my surprise.

The trick here is to provide an impersonal way for people to express their personal opinions. It may sound silly, but it does work.

I like to challenge the meeting participants to get themselves to a green cup. Influence the team with data to help you end up with a group decisions that you support.

Searching for and finding more helpful ways to think about how teams conduct their business can provide substantial benefits to the team members and their organizations.

BENCHMARKING

Benchmarking, in a business sense, is about comparing your own organization to "the best." How do you measure up compared to the winners?

While wanting to differentiate my organization, and not just "be as good as," benchmarking is also a method to help improvement and innovation teams to" discover what's possible."

With the helpful mental model of a process flow chart, later in this chapter, you are on a treasure hunt for more efficient and effective process flow chart steps and leading indicators.

PROCESS:

It is best to do this work with a team that knows their own processes well, is willing to learn from other process owners, in and out of their company, and likes developing the output to this process up on a wall with lots of flip charts and Post-Its.

1. **Identify macro-processes key to success.**
   Build a macro flow chart of your company.

2. **Analyze and prioritize key macro-processes.**
   Select the processes which improved would provide the greatest impact to your organization as measured by your Scoreboard.

3. **Identify key micro-processes.**
   Build micro flow charts of the processes selected in step 2.

4. **Identify key metrics for each micro process.**
   Identify and document key P/R measurements (leading, lagging indicators).

5. **Identify potential sources of information.**
   What other organizations in and out of your industry might exercise a process you're studying much better that you? Who can possibly show you "what's possible?"

6. **Determine how benchmarks will be collected.**
   Plan your treasure hunt by securing or building flowcharts of the process you will investigate. List your questions before you go. Make arrangements to tour with people who really know the process.

7. **Collect the data.**
   Use appropriate means to capture what you see: flow charts, run charts, histograms, procedures, videos, testimonials, etc.

8. **Analyze the data.**

9. **Establish improvement goals and action plans.**

10. **PDCA on process changes.**
    Treat data as you would using your organization's Improvement Process.

11. **Incorporate benchmarking into planning.**
    Proactively feed your strategic and tactical planning by selecting tasks in reference to company Scoreboards, industry benchmarks, etc.

12. **Keep looking over your shoulder.**
    Be open to learning about improvements wherever you may be.

    —Adapted from <u>American Samurai</u>, William Lareau

Please see the *Good Thinking Series: Imagine* to learn more about this tool.

CAUSE AND EFFECT DIAGRAM

Also called a fishbone for its appearance, and an Ishikawa Diagram for its originator.

This tool is primarily a brainstorming format to assist a team in documenting possible root causes.

PROCESS:

Volunteer to be the scribe who will enter team member ideas onto a flip chart sheet in the format listed below which everyone can see.

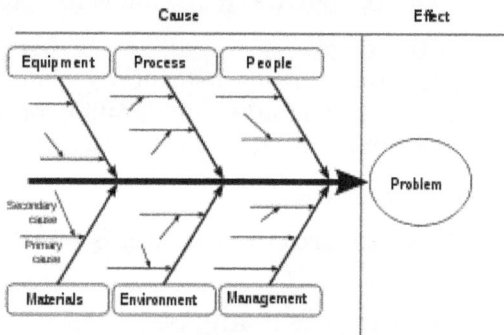

This is a free-flowing, open exercise where team members share their ideas. The fish-bone titles (equipment, process etc) are included on the chart before the brainstorming to focus the team on the most common sources of problem's causes. You can also use your own.

Starting with one bone, equipment for example, what are possible equipment-related causes to our current problem? As this first-level cause is written on one of the lines directly off the bone, you can then ask, "What contributes to this cause?" and write this idea off the first-level line as a second-level cause.

One version of this sequence is called the Five Why's. Ask why five times as you move through the sequence from a first-level cause all the way to a fifth-level cause.

Example - Problem: Plane late to depart

Brainstorming on the "equipment" bone.

- **Level 1:** Why is the plane late to depart? Maintenance need.
- **Level 2:** Why is there a maintenance need? Light went off on the cockpit dashboard.
- **Level 3:** Why did the light go off on the cockpit dashboard? Dashboard switch not operating correctly.
- **Level 4:** Why is the dashboard switch not operating correctly? Pilots often put their data binders on the dashboard while they're preparing for a flight breaking the switch levers.
- **Level 5:** Why do pilots often put their data binders on the dashboard while they're preparing for a flight? Binders are too large and heavy, and there is little space to place elsewhere.

This team would be encouraged then to move the pilot data to another provided surface or a small electronic device to eliminate the switch damage.

PLAN

The purpose of the tool is to sequence great questions that answered with data by the team help the team to discover what is, and what is not, contributing to a problem. Just because an item gets listed on the diagram does not mean it is actually a contributing cause. Resulting causes should be prioritized by likely impact and possibility, and pursued with further investigation.

Please see the *Good Thinking Series: Imagine* to learn more about this tool.

Communication Process Skills

We know that communication between people can be complicated. This series of paragraphs is only intended to remind you that you have to decide what happens when there is effective communication.

One common model includes the following steps and sub steps:

- Connecting: Building rapport, adapting, and using eye contact.
- Encouraging: Reinforcing, empathizing, accepting.
- Questioning: Open questioning.
- Confirming: Summarizing, checking.
- Providing: Stating benefits, speaking concisely, using enthusiasm.

Common supporting suggestions include:

- Listen actively and acknowledge what has been said.
- Speak to be understood; What method will be best received?
- Speak about yourself, not them. "I feel let down, not, You cheated me!"

- Speak for a purpose; speak only if there is value to speaking.
- Manage your emotions:
  - o Recognize your and their emotions.
  - o Make emotions explicit/acknowledge as legitimate.
  - o Allow other side to let off steam.
  - o Don't react to emotional outbursts.
  - o Use symbolic gestures such as an apology.

I suspect that this book's readers have been through a workshop on a method like this. While I am not going to dig into this process, in the spirit of continuous improvement, I would suggest that you bother to document your preferred communication process and repeatedly wonder if it's working for you as well as it might.

I recommend not having a set sequence to the steps above, but rather choose to use each step as necessary, and using each step at least one time in each meeting.

What is your definition of a good communication? For the purpose of this book series, mine is when dialogue supports individuals and teams to build great decisions with great support. Use whatever it takes—communication, dialogue—to exchange information and everything else between people.

All the dialogue techniques and tools here, the other *Good Thinking Series* books, and elsewhere are alternative strategies to support effective communication.

CREATIVE THINKING SKILLS

Truly new ideas often don't often result from "normal

brainstorming." It often seems that truly new ideas come from the "accidental" crossing of paradigms, mixing new ideas that just don't logically belong together.

The self organizing capacity of our brains goes to work on this new, unique combination and tries tirelessly to "make sense" of the novel combination. "Lots of ideas" is the wonderful by product. 90% will be thrown away, but 10% will often include ideas, never before conceived, which warrant further consideration.

Example Technique - Imaginary Brainstorming

1. Define the goal or problem: How can we improve sales on the xyz product.

2. Define the essential elements of the problem or goal statement: subject, verb, object. (we, improve, sales).

3. Propose imaginary replacements for one of the elements of the problem statement. It is easiest to start with the subject. One helpful characteristic of the subject is that it has to be able to think, to have a point of view. Wilder is better; wilder takes you to a stepping stone that you have not exercised before. Select by number of laughs.

4. Formulate a new problem statement, substituting one of the imaginary elements. After you get good at substituting subjects, then try objects, then both. How can aliens improve our sales...

5. Brainstorm the new subject's solutions. Be sure to listen to your imagination and record what it offers you.

---

1. Goal Statement: How can we improve our sales on the xyz product?
subject = we, verb (goal) = improve, object = sales

2. Subject Options
mice
aliens
liberal republicans
ants
termites
circus wire walker
six year old
Captain Kangaroo

3. How can **aliens** improve our sales on the xyz product?

4. New Subject's solution

beam me up
ET phone home
light years away

5. Practical Ideas

phone marketing
sell to home owners
market at bike races
show product in homes

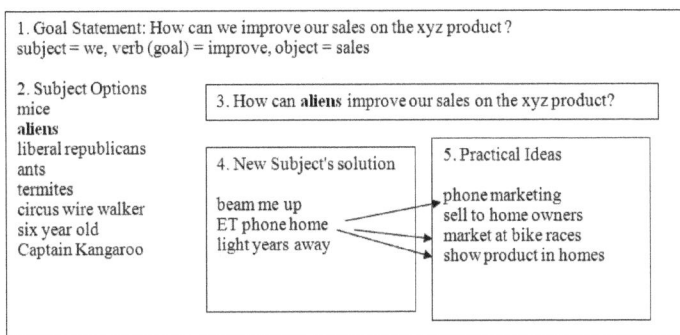

6. And now to make it practical. Apply ideas from the imaginary brainstorming back to the real problem statement. How can one of the alien's recommendations help you consider a new practical solution?

7. Analyze all of the brainstormed ideas (real, imaginary, combined) and further explore the more interesting ones.

I define creative thinking skills as the deliberate ability to generate new useful ideas. So these unusual techniques may not generate a 10 million dollar idea every time, but the ideas from these techniques likely did not appear on the first rounds of "normal brainstorming."

Please see the *Good Thinking Series: Imagine* to learn more about this tool.

CROSS-FUNCTIONAL PROCESS MAP

This tool's format clarifies cross-functional responsibilities of a process flow chart.

This tool can clarify how functions in an organization complete their work together. This tool shows relationships and sequence. The relationship diagram shows interdependencies.

PROCESS:

1. Assemble the people who most often do the w
at their place of work. Be prepared to gather
in the work place to document the process.

2. Identify the audience you are preparing the
ess flow chart for. How much detail do they i
macro (big fundamental steps), mini, (sm
fundamental steps), and micro (a level of c
which allows you to document root causes).

3. Complete the macro level flow chart.

4. Identify which functions complete which s
(bank manager, word processing, etc).

5. List functions on the y-axis of a matrix, with t
sequence along the x-axis.

6. Position process steps in the appropriate row
identify the sequence of steps with arrows.

EXAMPLE - LOAN PROCESS

This diagram shows both the macro level process flow
chart above the dark horizontal line, and the cross fun
tional process map below.

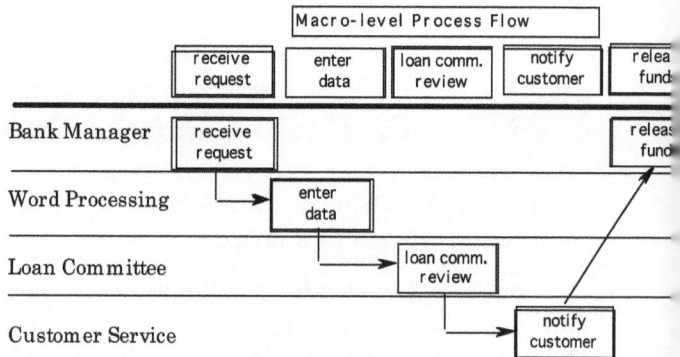

The first benefit comes from using this format to document current reality. How is the process really being conducted? Walk it through right in the workplace to confirm.

Then on another chart identify your preferred routing.

Doing this with either a white board or flip chart and Post-Its allows flexibility as you learn how things are, and how you'd like them to be.

Please see the *Good Thinking Series: Imagine* to learn more about this tool.

CUSTOMER RESEARCH

Successful business depends on the regular transfer of value from one company to another – from the provider to the customer. Knowing what your customer wants and will want is crucial to your success.

Establish and use a process to learn the "voice of the customer." This is one way to gather your customers' feedback. There are many sources and organizations who can help you dig deeper to help you learn what your customers would really like to see from your organization.

Serious customer research can include professional organizations able to solicit analyze statistically valid customer data.

PROCESS:

1. Prepare yourself for a "people to people" process. Study your customers history, their interests, and their company culture.

2. Document the combined process that you and the customer share – your process and theirs (with a value chain for example). Appreciate that your process is upstream from theirs, and that your cus-

tomer uses the outputs of your process. On this flow chart clarify your process's inputs and outputs, and the customer's process's inputs(your outputs) and their outputs.

3. Prepare and list the questions you will ask the customer to gain insights into the combined process and what the customer likes and dislikes about both your produce and your service.

4. Choose the method you will use to collect data. Options include:

   • surveys: phone, face-to-face, internet survey tools
   • focus groups
   • on-line research
   • user groups
   • voice mail

   Regardless of which method you use to collect a larger body of data, do visit a representative group of customers to confirm the data you collected.

5. Before you visit with the customer, practice your questions and interviewing process. It's best to discover what you like to do differently in a practice session with your own teammates, and not in front of the customer.

6. I recommend interviewers visit with the customer in pairs.

7. Meet with the customer at their facility. After introductions walk their process to see how your product/service is actually used by the customer.

8. Ask your questions and record your data.

9. Confirm your understanding of what you learned during the visit with a review of your data with your customer host.

10. Send a thank-you note and provide them a copy of your visit results.

11. Use what you learned from a number of customers to improve the processes that support your products and services.

DECISION MATRIX

Use to identify the most significant issue which when improved will provide the most impact.

1. Working with the same team that completed a multivote, construct a two-dimensional matrix listing the project options as row titles.

2. Use your scoreboard which represents the key factors which measured can monitor your success. Place these along the top row of the matrix. Example: QCDISM, Quality, Cost, Delivery, Innovation, Safety, and Morale. You may choose to weight these criteria to reflect their relative impact.

3. Select a scoring system to evaluate each process in respect to each criteria. For example, 5 = high impact, 3 =moderate impact, 1 = low impact.

4. Step through the project options evaluating and scoring each in respect to the criteria scoring system.

5. Lots of dialogue.

GOAL: Increase number of loans processed each month

Target Processes	Q	C	D	I	S	M	Total
Loan Request process	3	2	3	1	2	1	12
Loan Review process	3	4	5	1	1	1	15
Credit Check process	5	5	1	4	1	3	19

Scoring System: 5 = high impact, 3 =moderate impact, 1 = low impact

FLOWCHART BINGO

The purpose of this tool is to assist an individual or a team to wonder aloud about why a particular process is not performing as well as it might.

First: Document a currently troublesome process
Working alone or with a team:

1. Choose a troublesome issue or task that you are currently working on in your organization.

2. Using Post-Its to allow for corrections and flexibility, build a process flowchart for this target process.

3. Remember, this problem is a current natural consequence of a process in place. You may start by first posting the problem as the last step of the process, and post the preceding steps one at a time moving upstream.

4. Remember to include in your flowchart the processes of current P/R measurements; these feedback steps occur early (P = preventative) or at the end (R = result). These steps are posted diagonally to represent questions of "are we OK to this point?" See P/R Measurements in this chapter.

Note: It is important to document your troublesome process as it is, not as you'd like it to be. It is important to challenge someone's perception of how a process is happening. In the best case scenario the listener will not take the challenge personally; they will say, "That's how I see it. Let me show you." And the exercise party heads out to where the process is occurring and sees for themselves what's really happening.

Second: Document the flowchart's scoreboard

See Scoreboard in chapter three.

Third: Flow chart bingo procedures

Dialogue is a conversation that generates learning. Flow chart bingo is a dialogue technique that helps to discover which potential problems are located in which segments of a process.

1. Post your troublesome process flow chart on a wall so all team members can see it easily, or on a table in front of you if you are working alone.

2. Confirm that the flow chart represents the process as it currently operates. Correct if necessary.

3. Using colored dots, create a legend with your flow-chart's scoreboard that lists its preferred performance. Example: Red = quality, green = cost, yellow = delivery, etc.

4. Review your flowchart; compare each process step with each category of your scoreboard.

5. Place a colored dot wherever you believe a major problem occurs.

6. You will create a map of your process's waste targets.

The finished flowchart with a few concentrations of dots becomes a treasure map. Reducing or eliminating the issues highlighted by the dots represents eliminating waste. Eliminating waste is a spectacular money saver.

The history of quality improvement is based on the sequence of these steps: what process is causing the disappointment, what is the standard, what is the gap. Eliminate the gap and pursue the next troublesome process.

Please see the *Good Thinking Series*: *Imagine* to learn more about this tool.

FORCE FIELD DIAGRAM

An alternative brainstorming format. Use to identify significant forces which are restraining you from reaching your goals.

PROCESS:

1. Working with team members or others who know the issue best, write a goal at the top of a flip chart.

2. Brainstorm issues which promote the goal, and place them in the left column. Brainstorm issues which restrain the goal and place them in the right column.

3. Select a few significant forces that supported are eliminated will have the most impact when improved, i.e. the process to be assigned to an improvement team.

GOAL: Implement Improvement Capability

PROMOTING FORCES	RESTRAINING FORCES
customers demanding it	time
company leaders involved	budget
some suppliers can help	last initiative failed
training resources	morale could be better

FUTURE SEARCH

Future search is a planning meeting process that helps people transform their capability for action very quickly. The meeting is task-focused. It brings together 60-80 people in one room or hundreds in parallel rooms.

Future search brings people from all walks of life into the same conversation—those with resources, expertise, formal authority and need. They meet for sixteen hours spread across three days. People tell stories about their past, present and desired future. Through dialogue they discover their common ground. Only then do they make concrete action plans.

The meeting design comes from theories and principles tested in many cultures for the past fifty years. It relies on mutual learning among stakeholders as a catalyst for voluntary action and follow-up. People devise new forms of cooperation that continue for months or years.

Broad Applications

Future Search can be used to:

- Create a shared vision and practical action plans among diverse parties.
- Devise a plan and gain commitment to implement a vision or strategy that already exists.
- Initiate rapid action on complex issues where no coordinating structure or shared vision exists

People have applied future search in every sector in many cultures. Examples include affordable housing in Santa Cruz, CA, economic development among the Inuit people of North America, AIDS in Bangladesh, more effective business planning in Brazil, business mergers in Germany, sustainable communities in England, strengthening democratic practices in South Africa, regional planning in Indonesia, and education reform across the United States.

Basic Principles and Techniques

Four key principles underlie the future search design:

- Getting the "whole system" in the room.
- Exploring the same global context ("whole elephant") as a backdrop for local action.
- Focusing on the future and common ground rather than conflicts and problems.
- Inviting self-management and personal responsibility for action during and after the conference.

These principles, rather than any techniques, account for the widespread success of future search. You will learn in depth how they function to help people make better communities and organizations. You also will learn techniques that, taken together, put these principles into action, including self-organizing action groups and the critical interplay between small group tasks and whole conference dialogue.

Future Search Network has hundreds of examples worldwide. Please see *http://www.futuresearch.net/*

John Canfield has been trained to facilitate Future Search sessions by Sandra Janoff and Marvin Weisbord, founders of Future Search.

GANTT CHART

Named after Henry Gantt, (1861-1919) an American mechanical engineer and management consultant. Gantt charts were employed on major infrastructure projects including the Hoover Dam and Interstate highway system.

Use as a project management tool to clarify order and length of a project's assignments. The Gantt Chart highlights sequence of assignments and shows when assignments are serial or parallel.

PROCESS:

With the help of the whole project team:

1. List all the assignments and sub-assignments. This is easy and flexible with Post-Its.

2. Identify the required sequence of the assignments and place these steps in subsequent rows.

3. Identify which assignments must happen in series and which can happen in parallel. Two assignments in series shows that the first assignment must be completed before the second assignment can begin. For example (below), the team cannot begin to enter the data until they have completed receiving the request. This is shown by the project time lines in the two subsequent rows stop and start at the same time.

4. Two assignments in parallel, at least to some degree, shows that a following step can be initiated before you complete the previous assignment. For example, below the team can begin to review the loan before they complete entering the data. This is shown by the project time lines in the two subsequent rows overlap.

5. Present the assignments in the following manner:

EXAMPLE - LOAN PROCESS SCHEDULE

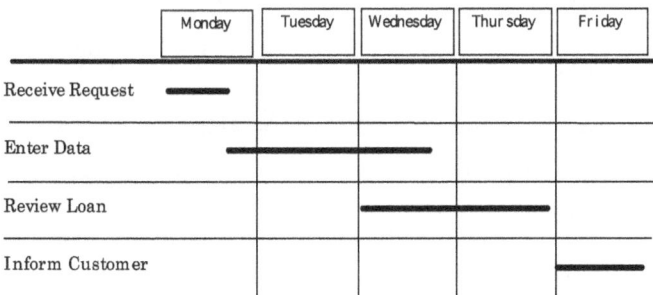

	Monday	Tuesday	Wednesday	Thursday	Friday
Receive Request	▬				
Enter Data		▬▬▬			
Review Loan			▬▬▬		
Inform Customer					▬

I prefer that the project teams uses the Gantt Chart as a dialogue tool, using the format to present, discuss, and place the assignments in the order the team supports, indicating the length of an assignment that the team agrees to, and collectively has the team ending the project assignment "on time."

Like other dialogue tools it's a great place to discuss with data about how long things need to take, and which assignment ought to follow or precede another.

Please see the *Good Thinking Series: Imagine* to learn more about this tool.

GREAT TEAM TRAITS

Great Team Traits provides a team an opportunity to consider, list, discuss, and prioritize the behaviors a team would prefer to see during its project work.

PROCESS:

AT YOUR TEAM TABLE:

1. Individually and silently brainstorm with Post-Its what your successful team is going to be like.

    What will success look like at the major milestones.

    Describe the journey and the arrival.

2. As with the brainstorming process described in chapter 6, have the team meet at a flip chart and present and discuss each person's ideas, one person at a time presenting one idea at a time. Con-

tinue placing and discussing until all the ideas are posted.

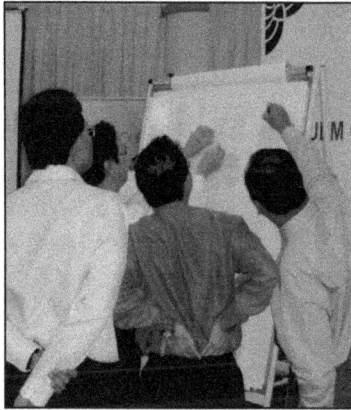

3. As a team, create an affinity diagram on a flip chart by sorting the team's Post-Its into "natural categories."

4. Write category headings at the top of each group. I'd recommend here to have the headings include action verbs.

5. Discuss insights about the resulting chart. "Does this chart represent what we as a team want to do?"

You have created a "Great Team Traits" scoreboard for your own team. Use it as a reference point when monitoring and evaluating your team's performance.

For example when it's time to assess a team's progress, direct the team's attention to the Great Team Traits flip chart and ask the team "How are we doing? Suggestions for improvement?"

Teams can also raise the bar. If they think there is an area for improvement, they can add new criteria they want to honor.

This is also a great icebreaker for new teams with the

advantage that you are creating a useful tool and not just talking about your favorite color or what day of the week you'd like to be.

IMPACT EASE DIAGRAM

An Impact Ease Diagram provides a simple flip chart format for a team to place brainstormed options/ initiatives (from a brainstorming session) on a grid to identify which they ought to do first (most often: easy to do & high impact).

The process is easy. Have the team brainstorm and post their ideas of how to complete a project on an open flip chart. Format a second flip chart as show below. Then have the team, facing both flip charts, pull one from the collection and nominate where it should be placed on the Impact Ease Diagram.

The team ought to support the placement of option. Discussion should be supported by data based positions, not just opinions.

Flip Chart Format

High Impact		
Low Impact		
	Hard to Do	Easy to Do

IMPROVEMENT PROCESS

The improvement process is an example of a systematic step-by-step method built by an organization's Leadership and Guidance Team for improvement teams to use to solve problems and build better processes.

Each step should include tools to guide the improvement team's learning. Each tool is another question. The sum of the answers should lead the team to identify the root cause of a problem and assist their efforts to build an improved process ready to be tested.

There are many variations available to benchmark. Automotive has what they call the 8 D's. Many companies learn the Kepner Tregoe method. A consistent framework for all these methods is the four groups of steps: plan, do, check, act.

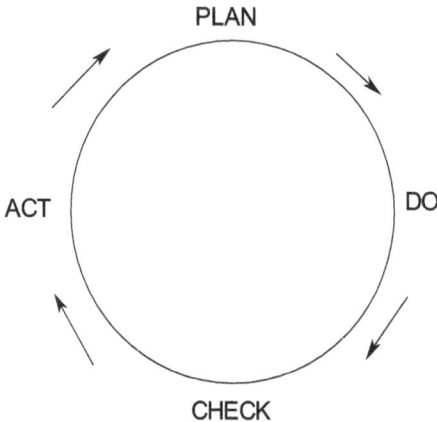

PLAN

ACT

DO

CHECK

These modern methods following the four major steps are often attributed to either Deming or Shewhart. Others suggest the framework comes from 18th century experimental methodology.

In any case, having the steps with the tools to follow, and the discipline to complete each tool seem to work very well. Modern versions include Six Sigma and Lean methodologies. Using similar methods to target waste and defects saves companies millions of dollars.

PLAN

EXAMPLE:

PLAN: identify your intended target

> 1. Establish Team
> 2. Define Problem Schedule Work
> 3. Describe Current Situation, Gather Data
> 4. Analyze, Prioritize Causes
> 5. Modify Flow Chart

DO: practice to generate feedback

> 6. Try Out Improvements

CHECK: compare feedback to target

> 7. Study Results

ACT: implement improvement and create next plan, or revise plan and start again

> 8. Standardize Improvements

PLAN: identify your intended target

> 9. Plan Next Improvements
>
> 10. CELEBRATE

Please see the *Good Thinking Series: Imagine* to learn more about this tool.

INTERRELATIONSHIP DIGRAPH

Use to identify which variable in a situation is the most causative, and is probably the best thing to pursue first.

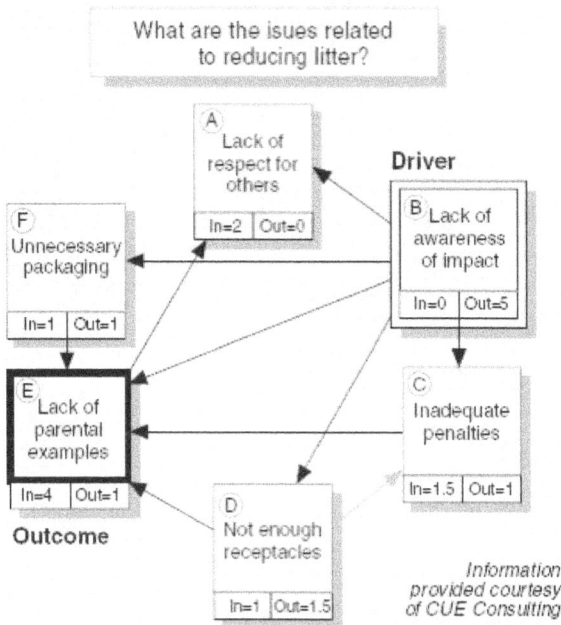

What are the isues related to reducing litter?

A — Lack of respect for others — In=2 | Out=0

Driver

B — Lack of awareness of impact — In=0 | Out=5

F — Unnecessary packaging — In=1 | Out=1

E — Lack of parental examples — In=4 | Out=1

C — Inadequate penalties — In=1.5 | Out=1

Outcome

D — Not enough receptacles — In=1 | Out=1.5

Information provided courtesy of CUE Consulting

1. Identify the problem or issue to be addressed.

2. Working with people who know the situation, brainstorm cause-components of the problem. For example, from the diagram above: lack of respect for respect for others, lack of awareness of impact, etc.

3. Arrange causes in a circle on flip chart paper.

4. Draw arrows between all appropriate issue-cards asking "which other cards are caused/influenced by this card?" The arrow points from the source of the cause or influence to the result-card in question.

5. The most significant cause has the greatest number of arrows coming from it; the best indicator of success has the most arrows going into it.

KANO MODEL

The Kano model can be used as a brainstorming format to help a team identify customer expectations, wants, and pleasant surprises.

The purpose of the tool is to differentiate product and service offerings. Done well it requires benchmarking and research to support the tool's brainstorming with data, not just opinions.

PROCESS

The original Kano Model will look like a graph with four quadrants with a diagonal line running from lower left to upper right. This diagonal line emphasizes that the expectations of customers improve over time.

Below the line represents basic attributes. The diagonal line represents performance attributes. The area above the line represents excitement attributes.

> **Basic Attributes** are unspoken but expected. Exclusion of these attributes in the product has the potential to severely impact the success of the product in the marketplace. An example would be any new car buyer expects there to be a spare tire in the trunk. That it's there is no big deal. If it was found missing, especially on a desolate road with a flat tire in the rain, it becomes a very big deal.

> **Performance Attributes** are those for which more is generally better, and will improve customer satisfaction. Conversely, an absent or weak performance attribute reduces customer satisfaction. Of the needs that customers verbalize, most will fall into the category of performance attrib-

utes. An example would be the mileage the car can get. Many car buyers are selecting cars based on their mileage. "Our car's mileage is as good or better than our competitors."

Excitement Attributes are unspoken and unexpected by customers but can result in high levels of customer satisfaction, however their absence does not lead to dissatisfaction. Excitement attributes often satisfy latent needs—real needs of which customers are currently unaware. In a competitive marketplace where manufacturers' products provide similar performance, providing excitement attributes that address "unknown needs" can provide a competitive advantage. Although they have followed the typical evolution to a performance then a threshold attribute, cup holders were initially excitement attributes. In New Orleans this is called lagniappe and means a little bit extra, like a baker's dozen—thirteen—one extra—free!

You can also use a simple format. On a flip chart, draw lines to create three columns with the following titles: basic attributes, performance attributes, and excitement attributes.

Then have the contributing team brainstorm, discuss, and place their data in the three columns, one column at a time. Lots of discussion, lots of data presentation. Lots of learning.

The overall goal of the exercise is to help the team confirm they are quietly fulfilling the customers' basic attributes, advertising and attracting customers to the performance attributes, and finally, with both the basic and performance attributes fulfilled, then providing something to the customer that pleasantly surprises them, encouraging them to select your product or service.

LEADING CHANGE

While leading a major change effort can be daunting, there are a number of resources that can ease the change agent's work and angst.

I first like to appreciate that any change effort is going to irritate some people. Some, many, people dislike change. I find the following a model helpful to consider.

The people you are going to include in your change effort will be in one of the four following corners.

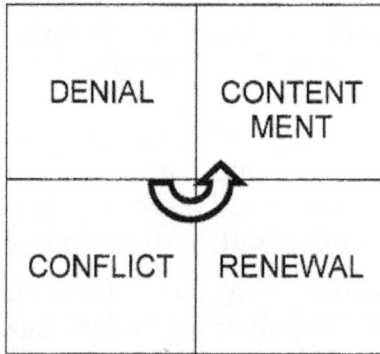

DENIAL	CONTENT MENT
CONFLICT	RENEWAL

Claes Janssen's talks about the four corners being apartment rooms. The model describes the states of emotion and thinking that your audience will experience.

While the goal is to help each person move from denial through conflict and renewal to contentment, it is important to appreciate that others who are in the other quadrants are there to begin with for their own good reasons.

A productive strategy to move employees is to ask questions, that answered by the employees, help them move into the next quadrant.

I like to combine this model with John Kotter's *Leading Change* series of steps. The book's chapters provide the detail to the questions of these steps:

1. Establish a sense of urgency.

2. Create a guiding coalition.

3. Develop a Vision & Strategy.

4. Communicate the Change Vision.

5. Empower broad based action.

6. Generate short-term wins.

7. Consolidate gains and produce more change - maintain the momentum.

8. Anchor the new approaches in the culture.

Kotter's steps 1-4 help people move from denial to conflict.

Kotter's steps 5 and 6 help people move from conflict to renewal.

Kotter's steps 7 and 8 help people move from renewal to contentment.

This use of a combination of tools is an example of assembling helpful questions that can guide the learning of a team that wants to improve and engage as many people as possible in the work.

MEETING PROCESS

Materials

- Three flip chart sheets. Place three flip charts on a wall near your table that your team can stand in front of.

- Post It pad and marker for each team member.

PLAN

Identify and Prioritize the Issues

1. Confirm that team members would like a more effective way to spend their time in meetings.
2. Use Post-Its with one idea per sheet. Silently brainstorm the negative characteristics of your recent meetings. Think about the speed bumps and roadblocks you'd love to eliminate from your meetings.
3. Meet at a flip chart. Working with one idea at a time, have each person put up their first issue. Talk about how the idea on the Post it slows down your meetings and affects your business. Identify, group and prioritize issues. Repeat till everyone's done.

Build an Effective Meeting Process

4. Silently brainstorm the positive characteristics of great meetings. Use Post-Its with one idea per sheet. Think about great meetings you've been part of. Think about ways to eliminate the issues identified in steps 2-3 above. All ideas written should be positive.
5. Meet at a new flip chart. Working with one idea at a time, have each person put up their first issue. Talk about how the idea on the Post it will help your meetings and affect your business. Repeat till everyone's done.
6. Place a third flip chart to the left. Write, "Meeting Process" at the top left of the flip chart, and, "Meeting Ground Rules" at the top right of the flip chart.
7. Using the brainstormed ideas, build a process flow chart on the **Meeting Process** flip chart along the left side, top to bottom, with those that *show sequence.*
8. List those ideas that *do not show sequence* under the **Meeting Ground Rules** heading.

9. Do include any new ideas as they occur to you as you work through this exercise.
10. Review your meeting process and ground rules.
11. Add to the bottom of the flip chart an area titled "Meeting Assessment Criteria" and list how you can build "self control" into your meetings.
    Examples might include:
    - Are we following the meeting process?
    - Are we following the ground rules?
    - Did we achieve the goals of our meeting?
12. Do benchmark other team's processes, ground rules, and team assessment criteria. Do they have any ideas you'd like to include in yours?

Build and begin to use this process with a small group that meets regularly. When you are dissatisfied with your meetings over a period of time, modify.

MOMENTS OF TRUTH

Moments of Truth is a brainstorming format that can help a team identify customer expectations as the experiences your products and services.

The purpose of the tool is provide a format to think about, document, and improve how an organization supports customers.

PROCESS:

1. Assemble the people who know most about your customers' interaction with your product and/or services.

2. Use a process flow chart as a format for your data collection and discussion.

3. Choose the start point and end point of the process you want to focus on.

4. List each process step as the customer would experience them. Represent process steps in boxes and describe with nouns and verbs. Post-Its are a good format for this work.

5. Include under each process step a prioritized list of what the customer wants at each step, and the degree, positive or negative, that you are supporting the customer wants.

To the purpose of robust dialogue, to find the truth, people should challenge any possible inaccurate assumptions. Try when possible to back up the data in and under the process steps with data, not just opinions or hopes.

The notion of "moments of truth" comes from Richard Normann, who argues that a service company's overall performance is the sum of countless interactions between customers and employees that either help to retain a customer or send him to the competition.

The idea was later used by Jan Carlzon when he was CEO of Scandinavian Airlines back in 1986 and described the idea: "That spark and the emotionally driven behavior that creates it explain how great customer service companies earn trust and loyalty during "moments of truth": those few interactions (for instance, a lost credit card, a canceled flight, a damaged piece of clothing, or investment advice) when customers invest a high amount of emotional energy in the outcome. Superb handling of these moments requires an instinctive frontline response that puts the customer's emotional needs ahead of the company's and the employee's agendas" (adapted from Shep Hyken, *www.hyken.com*).

This tool can help a team build a deep shared understanding of how the customer is experiencing a company's products and services.

MULTIVOTING

Use to identify the top three to five issues listed on a brainstormed list:

1. Complete your brainstorming list on a flip chart following the steps listed on the brainstorming instructions.

2. Re-emphasize the topic and make sure all the alternatives are visible at the same time; post scoreboard next to list.

3. While reviewing the full list, confirm understanding of each alternative and combine any that are redundant.

4. Number the remaining alternatives.

5. Divide the total number of contributing factors by three or four to determine how many "votes" each team member will have to "spend" on any of the alternatives.

6. Have each team member write down for themselves which alternatives they want to cast their votes; a person can cast up to half their votes to one alternative.

7. Stepping down each numbered alternative, the scribe lists the votes after each. Have voters raise their hands and indicate the number of votes with the number of fingers shown.

8. Circle the alternatives which collected the greatest number of votes.

```
TOPIC: LATE DELIVERIES

1- slow trucks      x
2-traffc      xxxx
3-road construction   xxxxx
4-late paperwork      xxxxxxxxxx
5-lost address labels      xxx
6-no map used      x
7-inexperienced drivers
8-product not ready      xxxxxxxxxx
9-service too far from shipping   xxx
10-shipping memos not posted   xx
11-conflding priorities      xxxxx
12-excessive inspection at dock
13-wrong product      xxxxxxxxx
14-truck leaves early      xxxx
15-customer dock not open after
3:30
```

15/3 = 5 or 6 votes per team member

P/R MEASUREMENTS; LEADING, LAGGING INDICATORS

Use to this tool to document and clarify the locations and metrics of your process flowchart feedback loops.

Feedback loops are questions within or at the end of a process flow chart that ask if certain conditions are met at that point in the process. If so, move on. If not, the feedback loop should direct the process owner to a corrective step.

Your goal is to identify and implement measurements that allow you to monitor a process while it is operating and prevent process errors.

Here is an example of a flowchart that describes how a product moves from the supplier, through an organization, and to the customer.

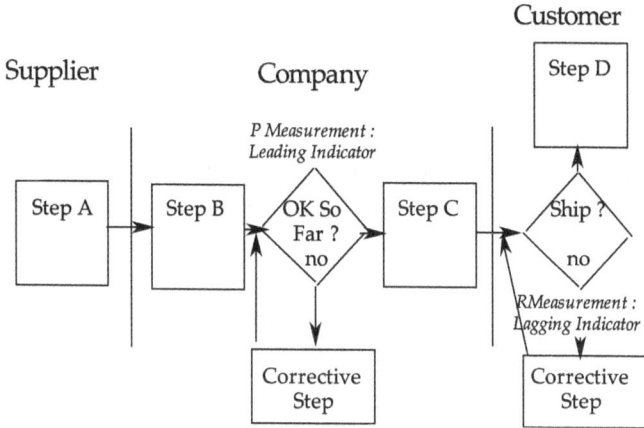

Customer

Supplier   Company   Step D

P Measurement :
Leading Indicator

| Step A | → | Step B | | OK So Far ? no | | Step C | | Ship ? no |

RMeasurement :
Lagging Indicator

Corrective Step   Corrective Step

For simplicity I have shown only two feedback loops.

1. After Step B, is the product good so far? No defects? No problems?

2. After Step C, is the product good to ship? No defects? No problems?

In both cases, if the answer is no, the product moves to a corrective step before it can re-enter the process.

Our goal is to provide a defect-free product to the customer. I would prefer to identify any possible problems up stream in my process so I can either prevent the problems, or catch the product from moving on if it is defective. It is helpful to have both P and R measurements.

Feedback loops upstream to prevent problems (P - **p**rocess, **p**reventative, **p**roactive, etc), and downstream (R - result) to confirm the product has no problems and is ready to ship.

An improvement team's goal is to place a sufficient

number of P measurements in a process to prevent any possible defects, and assure my preferred results at the R measurement.. A second level of P measurements can help me reduce waste.

Please see the *Good Thinking Series: Imagine* to learn more about this tool.

PARETO DIAGRAM

This tool helps a team identify the significant few, and the trivial many, when wondering which options to pursue—which are important, which are not.

This is often called the 80/20 rule. It seems to describe a principle that has you consider that 80% or your problems come from 20% of your customers, 80% or your revenues come from 20% of your customers, etc.

Many examples are available to consider on Google Images.

One way to develop a practical Pareto Diagram is to have a team identify a goal, say problems with a team's performance. Have people brainstorm with Post-Its all the possible causes of poor team performance, move them into an affinity diagram, and then take the groups, from the largest group, to the smallest group, and reposition the Post-Its into a stacked bar graph. With the largest group, start with the lower left of a flip chart, and stack all the Post-Its in a tall column.

Then do the same with the next largest group of Post-Its. Repeat until all the groups are posted.

You have created a Pareto Diagram which shows which cause of poor team performance has the most Post-It entries, and hence the highest bar in the diagram.

You would then be encouraged to target the first column's title to work on first to improve a team's performance.

The Pareto Diagram encourages you to identify and target the short list of to do's, and not distribute your attention randomly across a wider range of alternatives.

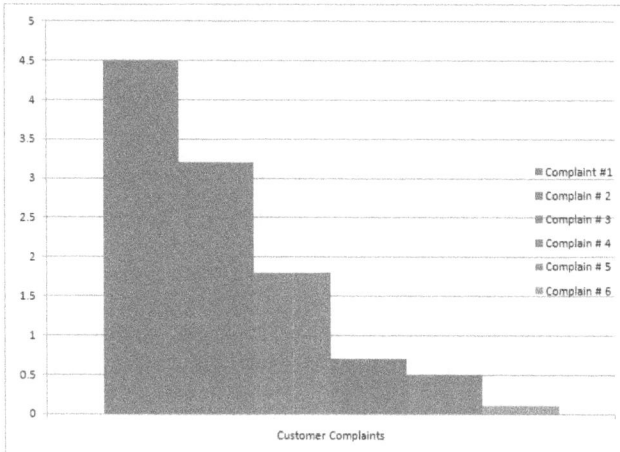

Customer Complaints

A variety of alternative problem solving solutions rarely provides the same impact; some most often provide better results, with less time, less cost, etc.

PRIORITIZING PROCESSES

PROCESS:

A. Document Goals

1. As a team, develop a SCOREBOARD to clarify what you want to accomplish.

B. Generate Alternative Solutions

2. Working alone to begin with, list each idea you have on Post It's. Then in an orderly manner, have each member of the team, sitting around a table or standing, share their ideas one-at-a-time as they place their entries on a flip chart. If a team member has no new entries, they may pass. If they think of new ones, they can get back into the sequence when their turn comes in the next go-round (nominal group technique).

C. Select Alternatives

3. While looking at all the alternatives, and considering your scoreboard, multivote your list to narrow it down to your top five or six choices.

4a. Using these top five or six choices, and your scoreboard complete a decision matrix.

OR

4b. Using your top choices, and considering your SCOREBOARD, place the alternatives on a IMPACT/EASE DIAGRAM.

OR

4c. Using your top choices, and considering your SCOREBOARD, complete an INTERRELATION-SHIP DIGRAPH.

D. Confirm each member supports the decisions these tools assisted you in making.

PROCESS DECISION PROGRAM CHART

The process decision program chart is a planning tool

used to identify and arrange the steps of a project's process steps and sub steps, anticipate the possible problems and consequences of the steps, and consider proactive responses to possible problems. It is a form of scenario thinking.

PROCESS:

1. Gather the team which will be affected by the process.

2. Identify the process and document with a macro process flow chart.

3. Gather 2nd level steps, What If's, and Possible Reactions information and arrange in the following format:

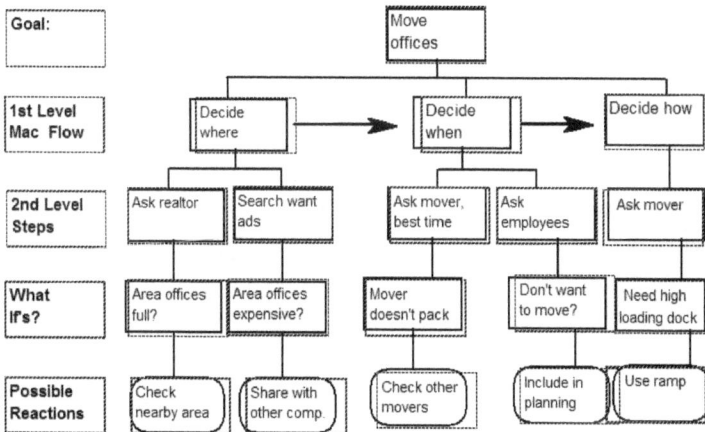

Goal:			Move offices		
1st Level Mac Flow	Decide where	⟶	Decide when	⟶	Decide how
2nd Level Steps	Ask realtor	Search want ads	Ask mover, best time	Ask employees	Ask mover
What If's?	Area offices full?	Area offices expensive?	Mover doesn't pack	Don't want to move?	Need high loading dock
Possible Reactions	Check nearby area	Share with other comp.	Check other movers	Include in planning	Use ramp

4. Openly nominate and post potential What Ifs (speed bumps and road blocks) for each 2nd level step.

5. Carefully develop possible reactions to the What Ifs.

PROCESS FLOW CHART

The process flow chart may well be the most useful tool for teams to use talk about how things happen, and how they should happen.

Process flow charts are visual maps that show the cause and effect steps and sequence of how work gets done.

Appreciate that the process flow chart format is another way to brainstorm ideas. The accuracy of the flow chart must be confirmed with data.

Process flow charts can be drawn at any level of detail. Here I am showing three levels: macro, mini, and micro.

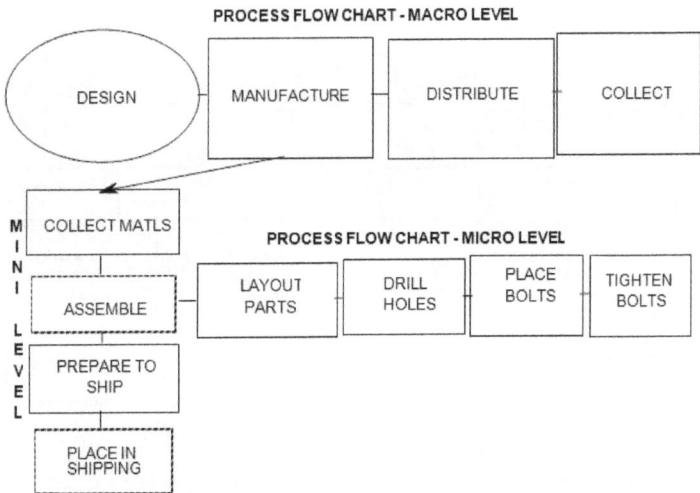

PROCESS FLOW CHART - MACRO LEVEL

DESIGN	MANUFACTURE	DISTRIBUTE	COLLECT

MINI LEVEL

- COLLECT MATLS
- ASSEMBLE
- PREPARE TO SHIP
- PLACE IN SHIPPING

PROCESS FLOW CHART - MICRO LEVEL

LAYOUT PARTS	DRILL HOLES	PLACE BOLTS	TIGHTEN BOLTS

- macro (big fundamental steps),
- mini, (smaller fundamental steps), and
- micro (a level of detail which allows you to document root causes).

When trying to solve problems, work first to identify how the work is actually being done by documenting the process where it's happening, with the people doing the work, and with data from the process.

If you're trying to solve a problem, appreciate that the flow chart you draw, if accurate, describes a process that creates the problem.

EXAMPLE PROCESS

1. Assemble the people who most often do the work, at their place of work. Be prepared to gather data out in the work place to document the process.

2. Identify the audience you are preparing the process flow chart for. How much detail do they need?

3. Choose the start point and end point of the process you want to focus on. Represent process steps in boxes and describe each step with a nouns and verbs.

4. Complete the chart and confirm for accuracy.

5. The conversation that develops this chart should be honest and robust. Using a flip chart and Post-Its allows flexibility for changes and improvements.

Flow charts would be used next to document the preferred sequence of new steps that would generate a better result.

Please see the *Good Thinking Series: Imagine* to learn more about this tool.

RELATIONSHIP DIAGRAM

A relationship diagram helps a team identify the components of an organization's system and the relationships between those components. This tool is often used when teams are beginning or reviewing their macro-level goals. Can be used in conjunction with a cross functional process map to highlight sequence.

PROCESS:

1. Starting with a flip chart, place "function boxes" of company functions (sales, customer service, manufacturing, R&D, etc.) in center of the flip chart. Using Post Is make this flexible.

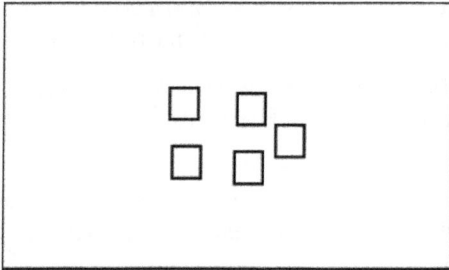

2. Draw a box around the functions that represent the organization.

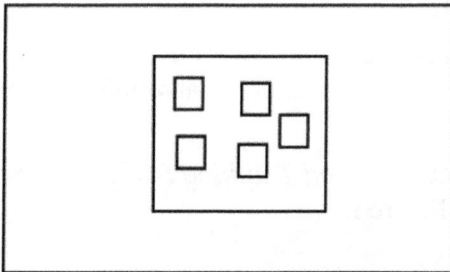

3. Place "function boxes" of company-partner functions (customers, suppliers, delivery, banks, shareholders, etc.) outside the box.

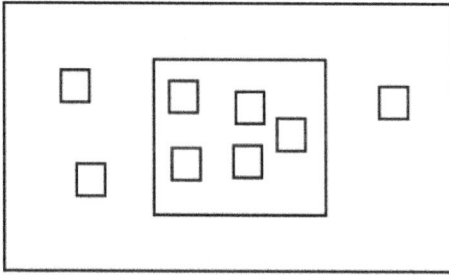

4. Draw <u>and title</u> single-ended arrows between function boxes to identify what value information, orders, money, ideas, capital, etc.) is transferred from whom to whom.

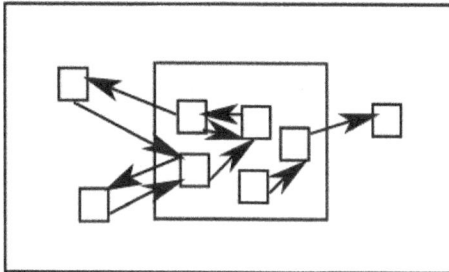

5. Discuss findings with team.

Like many other "current reality" brainstorming tools, the dialogue that helps build this diagram must be open and honest. When done, it's sort of like a circuit diagram. "Where are the shorts?" Where should there be a relationship line and there isn't, or where does the line represent a troubled relationship?

SIX THINKING HATS - Edward de Bono

A great tool to promote dialogue, Six Thinking Hats, developed by Dr. Edward de Bono, provides a practical framework that encourages the exploration of ideas.

In many organizations generating good ideas is a difficult process. When egos, emotions, information, and logic are all mixed together, the thinking process can become limited.

A story often shared in training circles is about five blind people who had never seen an elephant. The five circled the animal and touched it with their hands to gather data. When they shared their findings, the person near the trunk could only describe a long cylindrical object. The one near the feet viewed the elephant as a massive tree trunk. The third, who was at the tail, reported something all together different.

One option for this team would be to argue about their own points of view to confirm their findings and egos. Another would be to accept that, because of their point of view, they were limited in what they could learn from their own vantage point. They could appreciate their fallibility and open the conversation to all points of view, working to integrate these points of view into a single comprehensive understanding of the whole elephant.

Six Thinking Hats does a great job of walking a team around their elephant, around their issue, gathering useful data efficiently, with six points of view, while suspending judgment, promoting team learning, and helping the team to arrive at a shared understanding of an issue before they move toward making a decision.

The trick here is to guide a team's thinking to get ideas on the table while the team suspends judgment. De Bono suggests there are six types of thinking that you unconsciously use every day.

Each metaphorical hat represents one of those six ways of thinking provoked by a question:

- White Hat - What do we know and want to know?
- Black Hat - Why might the idea not work?
- Yellow Hat - Why might the idea work?
- Red Hat - What is your intuition about the idea?
- Green Hat - What are some alternatives to the idea?
- Blue Hat - Knowing what we know now, what should we do next?

Used correctly, the process encourages people to separate fact from opinion, to look fully at both positive and negative opinions and to get hidden agendas that can sabotage any meeting on the table. It stimulates their innate creativity and helps them discover how to turn seemingly insoluble problems into real opportunities.

Used correctly, the hats keep your different kinds of thinking separated, focused and controlled. They enable you to evaluate situations objectively by consciously switching in and out of the six thinking modes (hats). This process teaches an individual to look at decisions and problems systematically.

I have seen few groups who have only "read the book" realize the full benefits of this approach. I encourage you to find an experienced qualified trainer and learn to use the hats correctly.

See chapter seven in *Imagine* to learn more.

STORYBOARD

Disney gets some of the credit for this idea. In days

past they used story boards to have a flexible location to put cartoon drawings so reviewers can see how all the pictures fit together.

Storyboards can be used in companies to document an Improvement Team's work as they progress through their improvement process. As a team completes the work of each improvement process step, they either post the actual work, often on flip charts, or a summary review, up on the storyboard.

Best case the storyboard becomes the place where a project's leadership sponsors can go regularly to see how their team is doing without attending or micromanaging the project team.

STORYBOARD - IMPROVEMENT PROCESS STEPS   continues

1	2	3	4	5	6
Establish Team	**Define Problem**	**Describe Current Situation**	**Analyze, Prioritize Causes**	**Modify Flow Chart**	**Try Out Imprvmnts**
•assigned process	•brainstorm	•process flow chart	•brainstorm	•process flow chart	•process flow chart
•meeting process	•affinity diagram	•rel diag	•cause/ effect dia	•P/R meas	•checksheet
•impmnt process	•scoreboard	•value chain	•pareto diagram	•buyoff #1 meeting notice	•run charts
•leadership buyoff criteria	•Gantt chart	•cross functional process map	•decision matrix	•etc	•etc
•etc	•etc	•etc	•etc		

SYSTEMATIC DIAGRAM

Also called Tree Diagram, or Dendogram

Another brainstorming format, this tool uses a flip chart and Post-Its to help a team identify and arrange paths and tasks to achieve primary and supporting goals, or as a cause and effect diagram, effects and different levels of causes.

PROCESS:

1. Complete brainstorming exercise listing all steps required to complete project.

2. Arrange the steps in the following manner:

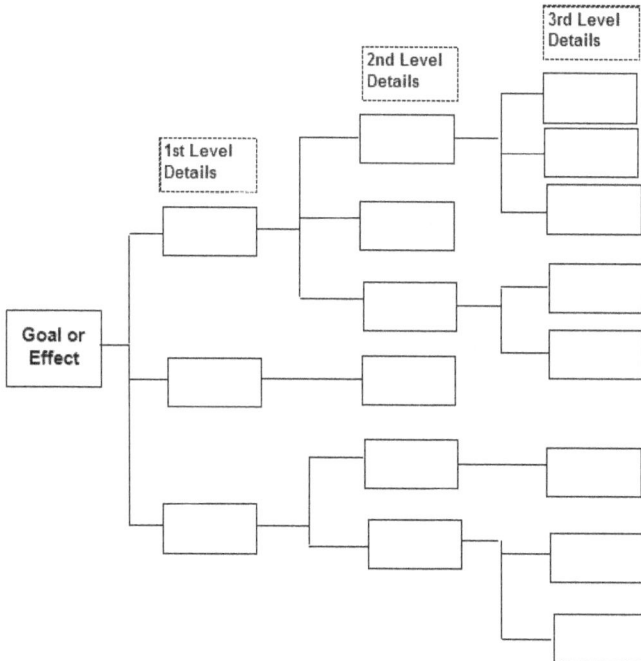

PLAN

THINKING AND PERFORMANCE

This tool and exercise helps a leadership team develop a culture specific listing of success-promoting and restraining thinking and behaviors. This exercise is based on a General Electric model linking an organization's performance with its' culture.

This is a data driven 180 degree performance review providing an opportunity for direct reports to assess their leaders. This tool's dialogue considers results but focuses on the contributing thinking and behaviors that drive the results.

PROCESS:

Randomly select the sequence of leaders to be evaluated. Work on one leader at a time, completing their chart before moving on.

Identify promoting and restraining behaviors:

a. Working first alone and silently identify and list *behaviors* of the leader on Post-Its, *one per sheet,* that promote or restrain your success. How does this leader help or hinder you in your job?

b. Working with your own list, pick your top three promoting behaviors, and top three restraining behaviors. Each person documents six behaviors per leader.

c. Begin a discussion with your peers, moving around the table one-person-at-a-time, presenting one behavior per turn.

d. As the presenter discusses the behavior, they explain their view about how this behavior promotes or restrains success at your company. Dialogue, dialogue.

e. Place behavior Post-It on matrix in appropriate quadrant.

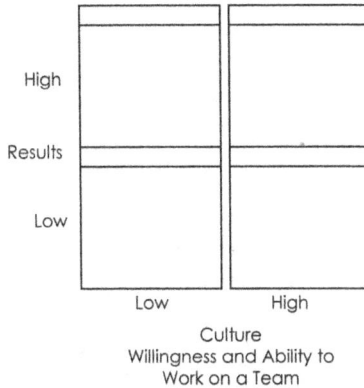

High

Results

Low

Low   High

Culture
Willingness and Ability to
Work on a Team

f. Continue until each person has placed their six behavior Post-Its. Tick mark duplicates to document frequency.

g. Take all promoting behaviors and create an affinity diagram; the category titles will be the parameters for the right side of your culture axis.

h. Take all restraining behaviors and create an affinity diagram; the category titles will be the parameters for the left side of your culture axis. Identify titles for your culture axis.

i. Finally, consider the behavior titles and discuss and document the thinking you think that drives those behaviors.

Best facilitated by a person outside the company who can neutrally collate and present the data to the leadership team members, one-on-one, and then the aggregate to the larger leadership team.

VALUE CHAIN

Teams can use a value chain to brainstorm, confirm, and document how value transfers between company and company-partner groups.

The macro components of a company's system are represented in the chart below:

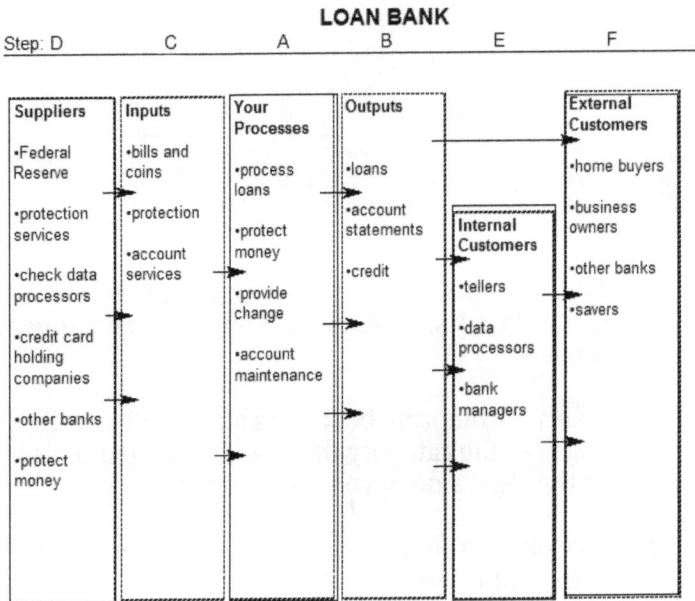

LOAN BANK

Step: D	C	A	B	E	F

Suppliers	Inputs	Your Processes	Outputs			External Customers
•Federal Reserve	•bills and coins	•process loans	•loans			•home buyers
•protection services	•protection	•protect money	•account statements	**Internal Customers**		•business owners
•check data processors	•account services	•provide change	•credit	•tellers		•other banks
•credit card holding companies		•account maintenance		•data processors		•savers
•other banks				•bank managers		
•protect money						

From left to right: suppliers, who provide my process's inputs, which my processes use to generate outputs (products and services) for both internal and external customers.

PROCESS:

1. Assemble the people who lead the functional groups and know the most about what their group receives (inputs) and provides (outputs).

2. Outline a system wide (company and company-partner groups) macro-process flow chart like the one just presented.

3. Identify and list the inputs and outputs for each group. Note column-step sequence:

This version has you:

- Start with your own processes (step A), and then...

- Ask what outputs (step B) do our processes produce (products and services). Then to...

- Discuss and capture the inputs to our processes (step C), and the suppliers to those outputs (step D). Finally to...

- Post the customers of the outputs, internal customers (step E) and external customers (step F).

As with other brainstorming formats, you want lots of dialogue and challenge to the many assumptions about how things actually get done in the system you are discussing.

WASTE SEARCH

Not too many years ago a manufacturer would have an "acceptable scrap" entry in his balance sheet. This pretty much accepted that waste was inevitable, and to keep it pretty low was a noble goal.

With the advent of teams using tools like process flow charts and improvement processes to really dig into how processes were really being conducted, many forms of waste have come to our attention.

For a company that cannot deliberately improve their

processes, this waste is estimated to be 10-30 percent of the organization's revenues. This waste is often hiding in company processes.

"There are many examples of waste in the workplace, but not all waste is obvious. It often appears in the guise of useful work. We must see beneath the surface and grasp the essence."
—Dr. Alan Robinson,
Modern Approaches to Manufacturing Improvement

One of the most famous searchers of waste was Taichii Ohno of Toyota. A significant contribution of Ohno's was his list of the Seven Sources of Waste:

1. Overproduction—too much of the right products or services; extra work.

2. Waiting - delayed action; forgetting.

3. Inventory; work-in-process - deteriorating products or services; un-used training.

4. Unnecessary processing—too many steps; no added value.

5. Transportation—excessive time or distance between stations.

6. Motion within work station—in our day-to-day jobs

7. Defects, errors.

The key benefit of lists like this is it provides a taxonomy to assist improvement teams in recognizing, understanding, and prioritizing sources of waste.

Another taxonomy useful with service producing processes:

Twelve Cornerstone Tools

1. Bureaucracy elimination : unnecessary administrative tasks.

2. Duplication elimination : identical activities.

3. Value-added assessment: contributes to customer expectations.

4. Simplification: reduce complexity.

5. Process cycle-time reduction : shorten cycles.

6. Error-proofing: Poka Yoke.

7. Upgrading : effective use of capital.

8. Simple language : easy for user to comprehend.

9. Standardization : selecting a single way.

10. Supplier partnerships : improve inputs.

11. Big picture improvement : systems view.

12. Automation and/or mechanization : free up people from routine tasks.

—Dr. H.J. Harrington
Business Process Improvement

Planning Sessions – Additional Considerations

Stamp Out BOPSAT – Collaboration and Shared Work Space

The more I facilitate working sessions, the more I notice how taking the time to set up the work area and supporting processes (collaboration tools), the bigger difference it makes in the efficiency and productivity of the meeting.

As with other collaboration tools, using the wall, posting data on flip charts creates common work space while reducing eye contact which often contributes to unnecessary escalating interpersonal conflicts. Using the wall focuses the team on the goals and ideas. Having people only sit around a table allows the team to regress to personal agendas and strong opinions.

In an online article on the subject, from Intellimeet (http://gointellimeet.com/blog/?m=201004), Michael Schrage, research fellow at the Massachusetts Institute of Technology and author of two critically-acclaimed books about collaboration, states that collaboration requires shared space, that collaborative thinking requires a space —be it a napkin, flip chart, whiteboard, or some other medium—where the collaborators are able to share their thoughts.

Schrage describes why collaboration requires shared space. Imagine a meeting of a dozen people in an office conference room. They are seated around a boardroom table. The group's meeting method is what Schrage likes to call the BOPSAT—Bunch Of People Sitting Around Talking. More precisely, people take turns talking. Schrage points out that someone talks, he is the focus of discussion. People look at him. People react to what he says and how he looks. The meeting is a carousel of egos, each grasping for the brass ring of attention. The group does nothing. He goes on to explain that the group does nothing because everything about the design of the meeting encourages individuals to make their points, not the group to create a shared understanding. There's nothing in the ecology of BOPSAT meetings that encourages collaborative creativity, problem solving, or decision making.

What's missing from the ecology of a BOPSAT meeting is shared space. Have you ever noticed how the character of a meeting changes when someone gets up and starts recording ideas on a whiteboard or flip chart? Everyone turns to face the shared space. People contribute their ideas to it. The combination of ideas begins to take shape. As Schrage explains, "The key is to create an environment that shifts attention away from the individual participant and toward community expression.

The key element, the key ingredient, the key medium for successful and effective collaboration is the creation and maintenance of shared space. You cannot create shared understandings without shared space." And someone needs to stand up literally and have the courage to change the arrangement of the workspace to take advantage of this significant insight.

Additional Resources

There are many books about strategic planning and scenario planning. I encourage you to pursue the best combination of resources, and tools and techniques, that serve you best.

Like a great buffet table, take what you will use. Don't try to learn it all before you begin to practice. The practice and the improved results will motivate and direct you to your next best tool and technique. In searching for other resources do consider that you are hunting for better questions. The questions are the change agents that provoke new thinking and resulting insights.

8
Prepare to Implement this New Thinking

"Every time a person puts a new idea across, they face a dozen people who thought of it before they did. But they only thought of it."

—Oren Arnold

One Thing That Will Remain the Same: Change Will Continue to Occur

As it's been said, "The future's not what it used to be." We experience change every day. In business, in our communities, in our homes, in our churches. Often change has a bad rap. We are creatures of comfort and don't mind things staying the same for a while so we can enjoy the good times, enjoy a rest, not have to think about it.

Competitiveness Requires Change

We live in a competitive world. Commerce is now global and for us to succeed we must be able to compete with, better exceed, our competition in providing products and services to our global markets. To compete, we must improve. To improve we must change. To change we must start doing something new, and stop what we have been doing that doesn't help anymore. One way to think about this has us deliberately substituting "improvement" for "change" at every chance. When we can operationalize improvement (change), when we can improve first and faster that our competitors, then we are acting proactively to secure our future.

Successful Change Strategies - Characteristics

What does it take to change a habit? Perhaps you have tried to change on a personal basis, whether your goal was to read more, weigh less, exercise more, or sleep less. Thinking back, just how successful have you or a loved one been in actually achieving the target? Successful goal achievers often report a laser beam focus on their goal, a discipline and schedule to the work to achieve it, honest feedback and encouragement, and a celebration of the new process that supports maintaining the goal. This is basic human nature stuff. People can change.

So now apply this to your organization:

- Can you think of anyone who hasn't attained their goal without deliberate effort? Do you know any organization that has improved accidently?
- Does your organization have a short list of key goals (to honor the Pareto Principle: the vital few and trivial many)?
- Does your organization have disciplined and structured support to guide this change (Change Agent Skills delivered on an ongoing basis to your employees/leaders responsible for influencing others)?
- Does your organization review feedback objectively in a regular basis to assess progress?

- Does your organization celebrate your wins on a regular basis? Are you changing and improving deliberately faster than your competitors?
- Are you satisfied with your process and results?

Successful Change Strategies - Assess Your Starting Point

All too often companies are pretty good at identifying ideas to improve and innovate but weak on the implementation and delivery. Good ideas get tackled by fear, pessimism, inertia, and politics. In my experience, what is needed is a special team of employees/leaders who are responsible for moving the ideas through the implementation stages. Many call these people change agents. Good change agents help teams make better decisions that more team members support.

Is your organization staffed with capable change agents? Can your teams make and implement great decisions faster than your competitors?

What a wonderful opportunity—to *not* copy your competitors who will "save money" by not continuing to develop their change capability—especially in tough economic times. One company hunkers down and weathers the storm. The other works through the rain and wind. Which company would you bet on when times get good again? It really depends on whether you see employee skills development as a cost or investment.

So What

Leaders who proactively learn about how things happen in teams, like considering options and making decisions, are better prepared to help their teams make great decisions everyone supports. Good decisions with good support is good business.

One of my primary insights after ten years in industry, (Intel and Herman Miller) and twenty years as an independent consultant around the world, is that thinking drives performance. Consider:

- Improved performance is the result of improved behaviors and decisions.
- Improved behaviors and decisions are the result of improved ideas.
- Improved ideas—breadth, depth, content, etc.—are the result of better thinking.

If this is close to true, considering the thinking that a leader uses is considering the DNA of their leadership and its effect on an organization. You could target behaviors and ask the suspect not to use them, but if you haven't provided an opportunity for the suspect to select new thinking, their behavior is likely to stay the same.

So, just how serious is an organization that says it really wants to be profitable, and a great place to work, but doesn't want to or cannot talk about the real source of the behavior? These nasty, unproductive behaviors are likely present in an organization that describes itself at the water cooler as dysfunctional. These nasty, unproductive behaviors are sources of waste right along the lines of Taiichi Ohno's famous seven sources of waste. So, it's OK in some companies to actively and deliberately pursue factory and process waste, but not OK to talk about waste-behaviors. Considering the enormous cost of dysfunction, this may be the next organizational performance frontier.

The chart below sort of captures my thinking about this performance and thinking link across a range of possible individuals. Read in columns:

Canfield's Attitude Matrix

THINKING	PERCEPTION OF THE SAME SITUATION				
THINKING	Mess	Problem	Change	Improvement	Competitive Opportunity
IDEAS	PERCEPTION OF ROLE				
IDEAS	Victim	Attendee	Participant	Contributor	Owner
BEHAVIOR	PERCEPTION OF RESPONSIBILITY				
BEHAVIOR	Blame	Wait	Manage	Proactive Do	Lead
RESULTS	BOTTOM LINE				
RESULTS	Awful	Ho Hum	Good	Better	Best

First of all, please notice the setting: the five individuals (columns) shown above are all sitting in the same situation. Yet their perceptions are significantly different.

The person in the first column sees a mess and considers themselves a victim ("My bad luck"). He or she reacts by blaming situations and others, and not surprisingly generates awful results.

The person on the other end, in the same situation, sees the light at the end of the tunnel. They lean into the opportunity, own the situation, lead their team, and likely generate admirable results.

In order for you to help build support for improvements, your thinking has to be in a good place. Considering the matrix above, where are you on an issue as you begin to influence others? What's the best way to think about this change issue in order to generate the behaviors in you that you need to support it? If you're not where you want to be, how can you get the information you need to be where you'd prefer to be?

My thirty years of industrial experience says that this is neither naïve nor simplistic. It is fundamental and comprehensive. Improve your thinking, improve your performance. And to my point of view, the column a person operates in is directly related to how they choose to think.

9
Next Steps

The *Good Thinking Series* of books is based upon the notion that improving thinking skills is the key driver to improving business performance. Thinking and intelligence are different. Intelligence is innate capability, and thinking is how you use it. As a skill it is improvable. What differentiates great and not-so-great companies is how they think, and how they help all their employees learn to think more effectively.

Improved Business Performance
↑ Implementation Skills
Improved Decisions, Behaviors
↑ Collaboration Skills
Improved Insights and Ideas
↑ Idea Generating Skills
Improved Thinking

Idea Generating Skills

All of these approaches/skills are supported by a wide variety of tools that guide a person or a team's thinking for a period of time to help generate better ideas. The tools don't tell you what to think, they tell you how so you can come up with more of your ideas that you like.

	Tactical	Strategic
Improve (Convergent)	Process Improvement Skills	Strategic Planning
	Collaboration Skills	
Innovate (Divergent)	Creative Thinking Skills	Scenario Planning

Core Topic: Collaboration Skills

Collaboration can be so much more than just assembling as a team to do work. Done poorly, the results are half-baked ideas sort-of supported by some of the team's members. Done well, the results are decisions that are better than anyone expected, supported enthusiastically by all of a team's members.

Productive collaboration includes the presentation of different points of view, and substantiation with data when possible. There are both ordinary and not-so-ordinary techniques and approaches which generate a wide variety of alternatives while deliberately building support for those alternatives. Effective techniques allow the team to physically place the issue out in front of the group, while minimizing distracting personality issues. Effective tools help teams build and support great decisions. Effective techniques promote better alternatives, better support, and better results.

Collaboration is the key skill set that drives effective teams to improve business performance. Supporting skills sets include idea generating, decision making, and implementing:

- **Process Improvement** targets waste, the 10-30% of a company's revenues most often being spent on unnecessary process steps by companies who have not learned to improve deliberately. Six Sigma and Lean are example methodologies developed to support these efforts. My comments have targeted those who are just starting.
- **Creative Thinking Skills** includes a wide variety of techniques to help individuals and teams to generate/provoke new ideas when they thought they may have had none.
- **Strategic Planning** helps teams develop an operational planning document that guides company leaders and employees, and improves the executive team's ability to identify, prioritize, and assign opportunities.
- **Scenario Planning** helps teams consider alternative futures. The value of this technique comes from the deep dialogue that the different scenario stories provoke. The alternate views generate new insights about a company and their future. Thinking this way helps prepare the contributors to notice and consider emerging ideas before others even perceive any change.

Added Benefits of Correct Use

What's really neat about the tools is when they are used correctly, they help a team avoid some nasty and money-wasting behaviors while they build both effective decisions and cooperative support simultaneously.

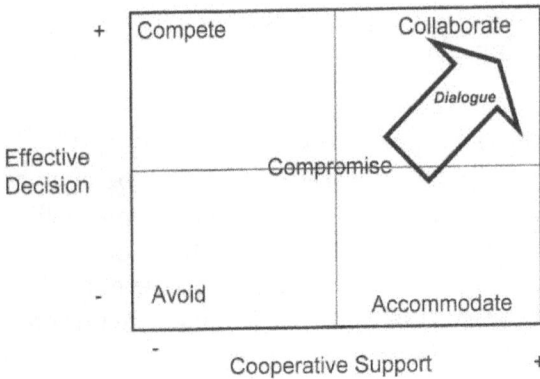

I define collaboration as the successful development of great decisions with great support.

Luck would have it that people behave in a variety of ways. A few behaviors restrain collaboration:

- Avoiders don't really want to help and have few good ideas. They often say, "I really can't help now, sorry."
- Accommodators are just in it for the fun of being together with others. When it's time to make a decision they say, "Whatever you say."
- The compromisers haven't learned to expect more. They settle for half a good decision and half the buy-in that might be developed. Their motto is, "I can live with that."
- The competers would rather do all this themselves. Their mantra is, "My way or the highway."

Our goal, collaborating, is different. Collaborating is all about learning a better way with a group. When these folks have two options, they've learned the best is always the third. Collaborating is a key business communication strategy to both improve and innovate. Settling for less than collaboration is a business decision, and often not a very good one. Using appropriate tools correctly tends to pull groups up into the collaborating corner.

The *Good Thinking Series* of books help you learn how to lead your teams into the upper right corner of collaboration by asking great questions that help teams learn how to handle their tasks in the areas of process improvement, creative thinking skills, strategic planning, and scenario planning.

Implementation Skills

Implementation skills provide the skills to support the implementation of great ideas.

	Current Projects	*New Projects*
One Project	Project Management	Leading Change
	Collaboration Skills	
Multiple Projects	Leading Teams	Leading an Innovative Organization

There are many good books available to support these topics.

My Favorites:

- **Project Management:** *Project Management Memory Jogger: A Pocket Guide for Project Teams*, Paula Martin and Karen Tate (Goal/QPC, 1997.)

- **Leading Teams:** *The Team Handbook: Second Edition,* Peter Scholtes, Brian Joiner, Barbara Streibel (Joiner Associates, 1996); *The Team Handbook: Third Edition,* Peter Scholtes, Brian Joiner, Barbara Streibel (Joiner Associates, 2003)

- **Leading Change:** *Leading Change,* John P. Kotter, (The Free Press, 1996).

- **Leading an Innovative Organization:** *Innovating the Corporation: Creating Value for Customers and Shareholders,* Thomas D. Kuczmarski, Arthur Middlebrooks, Jeffrey Swaddling, (NTC Business Books, 2001).

Next Steps - Select an Improvement Goal and Strategy

- Select a business goal that needs attention.
- Identify the behaviors, decisions, and ideas that you would prefer to see.
- What thinking approach and style would produce the preferred ideas, behaviors and decisions that would deliver the business goal you seek?
- Then find a resource to help you learn to think that way.

About the Author

John Canfield is an experienced business executive and coach who has been trained to facilitate a wide variety of planning, improvement, and innovation processes. John has many years of experience working and consulting in a wide variety of organizations around the world.

John has earned a B.S. in Mechanical & Industrial Engineering from the University of Minnesota and a B.A. in Political Science and Psychology from Williams College.

Prior to 1990 John was a Senior Engineering Manager for Intel Corporation and later Director of Corporate Quality and Design Research for Herman Miller.

To learn more about John please visit

Website: *www.johncanfield.com*

Article Series: *www.mibiz.com/goodthinking.html*

Videos: *www.youtube.com/canfieldgoodthinking*

LinkedIn: *www.linkedin.com/in/johncanfield*

• • •

Greg Smith is a writer, designer, and teacher. He collaborates on a variety of projects, in a wide-range of genres.

To learn more about Greg, please visit:

www.smithgreg.com

www.ingramcontent.com/pod-product-compliance
Lightning Source LLC
Chambersburg PA
CBHW020202200326
41521CB00005BA/219